PREACHING IN THE NEW AGE

Preaching in the New Age

An Art and an Incarnation

A Series of six lectures delivered in the Hartford Theological
Seminary upon the "Carew" Foundation in the Spring of 1900

BY
ALBERT J. LYMAN, D. D.

Fleming H. Revell Company
NEW YORK   CHICAGO   TORONTO
1902

Copyright, 1902 by
FLEMING H. REVELL COMPANY
(*May*)

INSCRIPTION

To the Students in our Theological Seminaries who, though representing various Christian communions, have, by their common and noble spirit, made these addresses possible, this little volume is inscribed.

March 6, 1902.

In the year *1873*, Mr. *Joseph Carew* of *South Hadley Falls, Mass.*, gave the sum of five thousand dollars to the *Hartford Theological Seminary*, for the purpose of establishing a Lectureship which should give the Institution free scope to conduct discussions of theological and related themes. In the year *1899-1900* the Rev. *Albert J. Lyman, D. D.*, of *Brooklyn*, delivered a course upon " *Preaching in the New Age,— An Art and an Incarnation.*" This series proved of great significance, originality and value. The Trustees and the Faculty are glad to have these vital subjects and their lofty treatment given to the public in a permanent form.

CHESTER D. HARTRANFT,
President.

FOREWORD

THE following six lectures, delivered in the Hartford Theological Seminary in the spring of 1900, were presented at the time with no thought of subsequent publication. They are not so much lectures as informal "talks," such as one might venture upon if speaking without elaboration, among personal friends. It is solely in response to the request of the students themselves to whom they were addressed, backed by the generous consent of the gentlemen of the Seminary Faculty, that courage has been gained to offer them in published form.

In compliance also with the wish of the students, the direct style of address employed at the outset has been retained upon these pages. The lectures (if one must have the hardihood to call them such) are reproduced with no material change, save in the omission of a few personal allusions and paragraphs of recapitulation. They make, therefore, no pretension to either the dignity or the studied finish of the essay, and are offered simply as a student's salutation to his fellow-students and to his comrades in the great work of our common ministry.

A. J. L.

Brooklyn, March 24, 1902.

CONTENTS

LECTURE I

INTRODUCTORY

LECTURE I

INTRODUCTORY

Our habit of mind does not welcome prolix intro-
duction. But, surely, on the other hand, no whim
of waiving formality or of saving time would excuse
the omission of one simple word by which I might
convey to you, Mr. President and Members of the
Faculty in this institution,—to you gentlemen of the
classes, and to you Christian ministers and friends,
who are present, my thanks for the honor you give to
me in the privilege of offering a few observations
upon one department of our common work.

I am no expert in the field of homiletics. Nothing
is further from my thoughts than to enter upon a general discussion of the theory and office of the Christian ministry. This lectureship was not instituted to
invade fields already ably occupied by expert professional instruction in the seminary curriculum. Recent
years have been affluent also in the production of
monographs upon this subject. On my own library
shelves, as on those of any clergyman, without special
attempt to assemble them, I count twenty such volumes or more, by the greatest masters of the art of
preaching in our day,—Liddon of London, and Dale
of Birmington, Stalker of Glasgow, and Watson of
Liverpool, Christlieb of Bonn, as well as Beecher,
Burton, Broadus, Behrends, Greer, Van Dyke Tucker

of our own country and, noblest among the noble, perhaps, our Bishop Brooks. To echo these masters were needless : to rival them impossible.

If you ask, therefore, for good advice about preaching, for rules, maxims, illustrative incidents, I simply, with a half-whimsical sense of my present limitations, point you to this row of books on your library shelves.

What have I then to offer worth a moment's attention ? Simply and solely this—that I may present one man's personal report of his own wrestle with a common task, as though I voiced a comrade's cheer in the rush of the charge to his younger associates who will be fighting when he falls.

My one endeavor then shall be to reproduce the point of view of the seminary student. My guiding thought will be to ask what would have been most helpful to me had I heard it twenty-five years ago. Nor can I be solicitous for that careful literary form suited to the oration or the essay. I am seeking to speak as I would in my own home to a younger fellow-worker, plainly, man to man. I trust that the adoption of this simpler method will not seem as if belittling the subject itself or be aside from the dignity of the foundation upon which these addresses are given.

It may perhaps be said also that these lectures do not enter the fields of apologetics or Biblical criticism. The irenic thought and faith of modern enlightened Christendom is not challenged. The position taken is that of a liberal but evangelical faith, welcoming indeed the spirit of rational critical inquiry as a part of the product of the Spirit of God working upon

and within the mind of man, but yet accepting also,
in common with the Church universal, the substantial
integrity of the main New Testament literature, as inspired by that same Spirit, and especially emphasizing
the divine supremacy of Jesus Christ, true Man of
men, and yet also Master and Saviour of men and
Son of God.

But the main introductory word is this :—My espe-
cial helps in preparing these conversations have been
you yourselves. It is the *seminary student himself*
whom I would summon to be the real lecturer in this
course, for, if I mistake not, it is in the mind of the
typical student and recent graduate that we shall find
reflected, as in a mirror, the true and vital aspects of
our vocation.

And this leads me to tell how I have been led to
choose this path of approach to our theme. Some
months ago, I had the pleasure to spend a few days
in this institution and enjoy the opportunity which
you freely gave to me of meeting personally the men
of the classes, and I ventured to ask them at what
points the problems of our great vocation were press-
ing upon them. I also asked a number of students in
this institution, and in other similar institutions of
various communions in the land, to write to me,
frankly putting questions as to what men now entering
the ministry most want to hear about and to know.
The answers which came back from the seminary
students I have collated and shall use them as a basis
for what I have to say. I have done this with a purpose which, if I mistake not, is in tune with a vital
philosophy of the subject itself.

For the Christian student of our day is himself a product of the most finely selected influences of Christian heredity in these ages, and, therefore, in the depths of the modern typical student mind we shall find the true picture of the vocation of the Christian ministry. How indeed should we secure a true statement, not of the mere technical outline perhaps, but of the spiritual content of a great art,—painting, for example, or music? Possibly not merely through learned monographs, nor even solely through technical instruction from professional experts. Might we not reach the heart of the thing also by consulting the fresher enthusiasm of the younger students of that art?

So and yet more of preaching. I would subpœna a thousand students from our American theological seminaries, and in their questions about preaching seek to find a true idea of what preaching should be. I am, therefore, venturing to reverse the conventional order of discussion. Instead of coming to the man from the standpoint of the subject, I will come to the subject from the standpoint of the man.

It were easy, of course, at this point to echo a certain too common satire levelled against alleged contrasts to any such elevated idea of the student as is thus indicated. In a superficial way of looking at the matter, seminary life may easily be identified with formalism, with traditional and perfunctory discussions, singularly learned and unconvincing, and a clever caricaturist can find his target in supposable instances of theological students who, by their immaturity, their conceit, their scholasticism, or their humdrum and mechanical view of their calling, belittle the calling itself. We can imagine a professor even without piety and a student without ardor and without humor, God's delicate test of reality and sanity; but to indulge in such persiflage is, I imagine, an odd waste of time, beside being foolishly untrue, for such allegations as these are, for the most part, to put it straight, a libel and a lie. The philosophy of sociological evolution refutes these libels. Their shallowness and falseness appear the moment we admit in any large way the law of heredity in modern Christian civilization, and add to that any vital sense of the meaning of Christ's promise to be always in His church and with His people.

I insist upon this. The time has come to do rational honor to that student mind which, however discredited, is in the next generation to direct the course of American Protestantism.

The typical student is more than an individual. We cannot dismiss him as a "theologue." To say "tyro" and "neophyte" does not state him or begin to state him. Professional fetters have not yet bound down his spirit; unfortunate experience no time yet to chill him; his own special peculiarities no opportunity to precipitate themselves into partial, rigid and unmanageable theories. On the contrary, parental consecration of the very parenthood that again has consecrated its child to the ministry, the struggle, valiant and patient, to pay one's own way, ten years of intellectual drill, "plain living" and at least thinking of "high thinking," the student's ardor, the scholar's ambition, the young preacher's passionate aspiration and self-despair, the mingled menace and attraction of yonder expectant audience, the authority of the ideal, the hunger to save, the vision of Christ, the sudden, thrilling dawn of a possible conception of our calling, so full of glowing life as to leave one half dizzy, so vital is it and so splendid;—all these influences working together have rendered our typical theological student not merely an educated gentleman, not merely a consecrated scholar, not merely a herald of the Cross even, but they have made him to carry in his own soul the true mirror and image of the vocation itself which he has chosen.

You will discount these phrases as savoring of wordy exaggeration. But I give you back "a Roland for your Oliver" and discount your discount. To state my point truly I must state it strongly.

Let us then analyze what the student sees and feels concerning preaching. Out of the perhaps one hundred questions from students to which I have referred, I have selected and, by your permission, will read forty-four. I would gladly read them all, but time is short and those which I omit are largely duplicates of those which I read. Every one of the citations is a literal quotation, without the change of a line, from these words and letters of theological students now in our seminaries, and I will quote not continuously from the same man or the same letter, but arrange the questions in a certain order of approach to our theme.

(1) "What do men expect from a preacher to-day?

(2) "What is the message which this age needs?

(3) "While the fundamental elements of the gos-

pel message are the same to-day as ever, does not this age demand to have certain of these elements emphasized more than others? If so, which?

(4) "How much apologetics is needed in the present preaching?

(5) "May one assume practical intellectual agreement with himself in his audience till the contrary is shown?

(6) "To what extent can the modern minister use the tone of authority formerly common?

(7) "How far ought one to recognize the demand sometimes heard that ministers inform the people as to the present status of Biblical criticism, and do the people care for such information?

(8) "How far can we get outside of the questions of higher criticism? How can we get right down to business?

(9) "How shall we make men realize that the authorship of Isaiah or the exact duration of future punishment are questions which do not determine their own immediate present duty to God and to society?

(10) "Is it important practically that the preacher should make clear his own view of inspiration as between the extreme "dictation" on the one hand and the purely naturalistic view of inspiration on the other? Can most people upon this and similar issues be trusted to take a *via media* without special discussion of the points at issue?

(11) "How can one preach a system of doctrine? Is it best to develop a system in successive sermons from week to week?

(12) "What should be the relation of one's theological system to the sermons?

(13) "How can the effect of the sermons be made cumulative, each sermon playing into the next so that the force of the continued preaching may work towards constant building of Christian character?

(14) "Does modern preaching emphasize the human side of the Person of Christ too much?

(15) "What has become in modern preaching of the personal appeal to the unconverted?

(16) "How can I reach the unrepentant sinner in the congregation?

(17) "How can the preacher reach the hearers who say the sermon is good but who make no effort to comply with it?

(18) "How can the preacher touch the practical, hard-headed business man in middle life who has lost the ideals which he cherished in his youth and yet who is an honest, honorable, public-spirited citizen but not a church member?

(19) "What will rally to the Church a larger percentage of men?

(20) "How are young men to be led to the Church and its work?

(21) "How can the children in a congregation be held by the same sermon which is for older people?

(22) "To what extent can the force of personal sympathy be made available in the pulpit?

(23) "What should be the relation of the preacher to social problems and political issues?

(24) "To what extent shall the young preacher

use his own experience, what he has had, as a source of illustration in the pulpit?

(25) "How shall one get personal experience into sermonic form?

(26) "How can a man find the common ground between himself and the congregation?

(27) "How shall a man sink out of sight so that men shall feel that they are not spectators of a human performance but listeners to a divine message?

(28) "Can you give us a relief picture of the arena in which we have our task?

(29) "What I want is something objective—a clear analysis of the conditions of society, the actual force of the environment upon which the preacher must make his impression.

(30) "I want perspective, not merely to know the factors of preaching, but to know them in due proportion and perspective, so as to emphasize the important and let the unimportant go.

(31) "How shall I, first, know the environment; and, secondly, know myself in adaptation to it?

(32) "In our seminary we would like to hear something definite and strong about the weapons we have to use,—both the certainties of truth which will be most effective, and also the intellectual resources which are most called into play.

(33) "I have a latent, vague feeling of misgiving in my ignorance as to what truth can be made most effective. I want information on definite points:— How long to preach?" (Which recalls the response of the Scotch professor when asked that question: "A half hour, with a leaning to the side of

mercy.")   "How much illustration to use?   How definite shall the application be?   Shall one directly aim at individuals?

(34)   "As I meet my fellow-students in our institutions, I become aware of a common feeling of a certain hopelessness in view of the vastness and variety of the preacher's duty.

(35)   "How shall I best analyze myself in relation to preaching?

(36)   "What are the qualities and powers to rate highest in taking an inventory of one's resources?

(37)   "I want to know what I ought to want in preaching?

(38)   "Knowing the real sociological conditions does not seem to encourage and help me much.   I want to know more about the secret of power in my message.

(39)   "I know my message; I do not know the field.   We get in the seminary the analysis of the message, and of ourselves in part.   What I want is knowledge of the field from the man who has been there.

(40)   "I want more vital touch with the life side of preaching.

(41)   "What I want is to know how to translate my own natural way of expressing the truth into such a way of expressing it as shall be telling and winning in effect upon the people I am speaking to.

(42)   "How shall I put what seems vital truth to me in the way I naturally put it, so it shall seem vital truth to John Smith in the pew yonder, in the way John Smith naturally expresses himself?

(43)   " Can a man definitely count upon receiving special aid from on high in addition to the natural powers of his own mind ?

(44)   " How can I realize three things :—1st. The field in which I have to work,—what people are really thinking and feeling ?   2d. What I have in myself ? 3d. How the Holy Spirit might be supposed to in- fluence the mind, and how shall one render due obedience to the impression thus conveyed ? "

I do not know what may be thought of these ques- tions.   To me they seem to be quite the most re- markable series of interrogatories from candidates for a calling, concerning that calling itself, which I have ever seen.   You will mark the curiously complete *en- semble* of the questions, so varied in form, yet so completely pervaded by a common inner spirit.

Are they merely questionings ?   They seem to me to be very much more.   They denote a certain atti- tude of the modern student's mind, touched at once with the spirit of the modern time and the spirit of Jesus, at once bowed by the majesty and fired by the fascination of a supreme vocation as it presents itself under living, current forms.

But more than this.   Am I in error in believing that one sees revealed in these questions the true line- aments of our vocation itself ?   Not so much the homiletic science thereof ; not so much the profes- sional technique thereof, but the vital content thereof, the humane and holy *genius* of our calling.   We are then to analyze what we find here in order to obtain our working definition of Christian preaching.

And first we set aside for the moment certain elements which are so general as not to appertain specifically to preaching, because equally applicable to other forms of Christian service.

A didactic element, for example, is of course present and ever preeminent in preaching. Preaching is teaching; but so is Sunday-school instruction teaching, or ought to be; so are seminary lectures teaching; so are tracts teaching, occasionally; but they are not preaching. Expounding the Scriptures may be preaching, or it may not be. So in the opposite direction. A hortatory element enters into preaching. Preaching is exhortation; but so is a private interview with a friend.

Segregating then that which applies solely to preaching, we find the elements which are paramount in the student's view of his vocation to divide themselves into two main groups of factors. The first of these groups of factors relates to preaching as an *art*—a practical art.

The student looks out upon his calling as involving at its supreme moment a wrestle with an audience. He sees in his mind's eye a thousand men waiting, careless, callous, dizzy with the week's whirl, dead in sins. In front of them the preacher asks himself—"What is preaching? Telling these men what I think?" Why, yes, in a sense. But that alone is like talking to a fish instead of fishing for him. Preaching is not soliloquy. What then is preaching? Stating what the Bible tells? Yes, certainly, for the Biblical thought is the thought of the Infinite disclosed through the divinely selected and inspired human development of a special race for a thousand years.

But even this by itself is not preaching, so runs the student's thought. Preaching is telling all this *so* that it will reach men, so that it will convince, persuade, win, save some among that thousand men. In other words, preaching is an *art*,—the supreme form of that highest art of man, the art of the orator, the art of persuasion, the art of so stating the truth as to make the hearer's attitude towards it identical with that of the speaker; the art of roused manhood in fit public action, to the end of winning, through speech, his fellow-men. As an illustration of this read, if you please, that wonderfully vivid description of the preaching of Thomas Chalmers, contained in a short essay on Chalmers by Dr. John Brown of Edinburgh.

But recurring again to our forty-four questions, what more do we find? Every one must see that this thought of preaching, as an art, even the noblest, is not the sole or even the chief factor in the student's conception. Back of the art lies another group of factors, far grander and more spiritual. How shall we entitle this second group? I venture to indicate the genius of the answer by using reverently that rich, divine word—Incarnation.

For if I do not misread the intuition of the student mind, it is to the effect that a genuine Christian ministry is in the very heart of it, in some degree a reincarnation of the Truth and Spirit of Christ. It is more than a report of the truth; it is a living presentment of it—an embodiment of it. Preaching is in the *man*, not in the sermon alone or chiefly. Preaching must have living body and movement. It must in-carnadine the otherwise statuesque and pallid didactic elements. It must, under human limitations, reincarnate something of the great Incarnation.

In this glowing and profound conception of preaching as a reproduction of Christ, mere professionalism sinks out of sight; mere art is forgotten. Didactic utterance seems to be only the outer vestibule for this vivid and vital thing, in which the eternal *Word*— the Son of God—becomes Himself reproduced, in some dim sign and token at least, in the word of man, in the roused, human personality which pours itself into the spoken syllables.

In this intuition as to the true spiritual content and method of Christian preaching, the profounder biology and the profounder philology unite. The deeper philosophy of life in its relation to language is in-voked. Intellectual processes, literary structure, vocal utterance, manner, gesture, all become moulds which the nimble and fluent personal spirit at once creates and fills, so that the result suggests at least, if God will, the tone, the cadence, the spirit of the Man of Calvary, the Christ of God.

As this idea reveals itself to the reverent young preacher, sentences of Scripture which had been mere mystical phrases, like silent mist-covered geyser pools, start out and up from the page into new and com-manding life.

[1] Matthew 10 : 20.—"It is not ye that speak, but the spirit of your Father that speaketh in you."

[1] The citations are from the "American Revision" of the N. T.

John 16 : 13.—"When He, the Spirit of truth, is come, He shall guide you into all the truth." 14th verse—"He shall take of mine and shall declare it unto you."

Acts 6 : 15.—"All that sat in the council, fastening their eyes on him, saw his face as it had been the face of an angel."

First letter to Corinth, 2 : 16.—"We have the mind of Christ."

Galatians 2 : 20.—"Christ liveth in me."

Second letter to Timothy, 1 : 14.—"The Holy Spirit which dwelleth in us." 4: 17.—"The Lord stood by me, and strengthened me; that through me the message might be fully proclaimed."

These are not merely first century specialties and refinements of apostolic prerogative; they are of the midmost life of all genuine Christian preaching in every age.

But this is not the end. These two great groups of factors in preaching, that which makes of it an art, and that which makes of it a true spiritual reincarnation of the Eternal Word, are not sharply severed and separated, but shade into each other, only with the spiritual factors always in the ascendant.

Art, in any lofty philosophy of it, shades up into the spirit of the incarnation itself, through its emphasis upon the element of *beauty*. A noble art in preaching passes up inevitably through the medium of beauty into the apprehension of that "*grace*," that charm of spiritual loveliness, that beauty of moral movement, which is the peculiar and winning trait of the supreme incarnation in Jesus Christ, and is also the supreme charm of true preaching, as distinguished from other forms of public address. The final impulse of a noble art by which truth seeks to disclose itself in forms of beauty so as to win the mind, rises, without a break, into the holy passion to reproduce the " grace " of Christ, so as to save the soul. Thus is produced a certain special and vital tone in preaching, the tone best suited at once to attract and to win, a rational earnestness, blended with a swift, glad grace, —a tone beautiful and holy, like music on Olivet after the Resurrection.

At this point we arrive then at what for the present purpose may serve as our definition of the idea of preaching. Following the analysis of what we discover in the depths of the student mind, we reach that working description of preaching which will control the following five simple addresses in this course. And we venture thus to phrase our idea.

Christian preaching in its unique distinction, involves the blending of an art and an incarnation—the noblest art and the purest incarnation, yet so as that the separate sense of the art disappears in the superior and sacred urgency of the incarnation.

This definition, to call it such, is not, of course, exhaustive. It is not technically scientific, and would hardly be admissible in a work on homiletics. It simply aims to render back to you in outline the vital consciousness of your own minds upon this subject.

But not even here is the analysis quite ended.

Recurring again to our forty-four questions, we discover this further apprehension pervading them, that true preaching is an incarnation in this sense

also, that it relates itself to every special age or fresh
social environment, in a certain style and form derived
from that age and suited to that environment.

And this subtle and pervasive quality which makes
true preaching ever *en rapport* with the age, incorpo-
rates itself in preaching, considered *both* as an art and
as an incarnation. For the genius of art, while
always true to certain immortal ideals, yet ever seeks
to render forth those ideals in the finest tone of the
current time, while, on the other hand, the genius of
the Christian incarnation is this—if I may be per-
mitted to quote from a former address which I had the
honor to make at your seminary commencement in
1897—"the principle of embodying a higher spirit in
the finest forms of a lower environment, for the sake
of lifting the whole of that environment to a higher
level."

The question therefore rises into an instant and
commanding importance :—What, at the heart of it,
and in the essence of it, is this new age, this novel,
daring, critical present age as differentiated from other
ages, or an advance upon them? To what new
rhythm is the spirit of man marching to-day? What
is the characteristic, what the mastering note, in the
thoughts, in the motives, in the errands of modern
life and modern society, and how shall preaching,
both as art in speech and as a Christian incarnation,
relate itself to these new currents of thought, of motive,
and of errand?

For it is possible, and even probable, that this
present age, by its peculiar ideas and ideals, by its
new tones and forces, is bringing these two aspects

of preaching, the artistic and the sacramental, into closer union, as well as finer relief, than has ever been witnessed before.

This, of course, will come up for discussion later on, and is a blessed and prophetic thing.

Here, then, fairly on and just within the threshold, we leave our theme to-night. The current talk of the waning power of the pulpit is a specious fallacy. What is true is simply the waning power of certain pulpit types that ought to wane. Men chatter of the passing away of eloquence. Nonsense ! It is only the passing away of grandiloquence. True eloquence is manhood in action—the soul on fire and in fit utterance—and that is never out of style.

Here, then, fellow students, is our scheme or rather your scheme in the outline of these forthcoming familiar addresses—yours, I say, rather than mine ; for I am simply articulating what, coming as near to you as I can, I have seemed to hear as the voice of your own minds.

I conclude, therefore, this initial word with the announcement of the five titles for the lectures, if one must call them such, which are arranged to follow.

For the second lecture,

Preaching an Art.

3d.   Preaching an Incarnation.

4th.   The New Age and its Relation to Preaching.

5th.   The Preacher of To-day Preparing his Sermon.

6th.   The Preacher of To-day before his Congregation.

LECTURE II

PREACHING AN ART

LECTURE II

PREACHING AN ART

In the consideration of this special topic we must at the outset put in a good-natured demurrer against easy misconception. All separate discussion of preaching as an art is liable to be misunderstood, as though art were the element supposed to be chiefly emphasized in pulpit speech; whereas, in our view, art holds but the second place. Yet it is really present.

Art in preaching not only "conceals" itself, but forgets itself at the moment of utterance, "the best action being involuntary," as Theodore Christlieb finely says. Yet art is indispensable and is the natural path of that professional discipline which leads up to the higher factors in pulpit address. The case against art in the pulpit, briefly stated, is this:—Preaching is practical. It is always supremely a wrestle to save, in the large sense of saving. It echoes the message of the Most High. It is not the dramatic imitation of passion; it is the passion itself. It seeks not chiefly to please, as mere art may do, but to inform, to convince, to win its hearers. Its chief constituent is spiritual reality. It issues in definite appeal and its main concern is to urge that appeal effectively. To suggest art in a business so sacred and instant seems shallow impertinence.

So strong is this way of putting the case, and so

33

precipitate the recoil from the notion that preaching is an art, however fine, that not in a single one of the courses of lectures recently given upon this subject in our seminaries, do I recall any full recognition of what the art-element really is in preaching. Even so supreme a preacher and expositor of preaching as Bishop Brooks forbids art in the pulpit. In his noble "Lectures on Preaching," he remarks:—"The definite and immediate purpose which a sermon has set before it makes it impossible to consider it as a work of art." Let me quote a little further from the uncompromising sentences of the great preacher of "Trinity" upon this point, for I would do utter justice to the prejudice against art in preaching; and if the prejudice has the better reason of the case I should wish that it, and not my simple plea on the other side, might be remembered. " It (the sermon) knows no essential and eternal type, but its law for what it ought to be comes from the needs and fickle changes of the men for whom it lives. Now this is thoroughly inartistic. Art contemplates and serves the absolute beauty. The simple work of art is the pure utterance of beautiful thought in beautiful form without further purpose than simply that it should be uttered. . . . Art knows nothing of the tumultuous eagerness of earnest purpose." It might be fairly questioned, perhaps, whether such a wholesale verdict as this is consistent with the truest view of art, or with the history of art in the world. Not only in the fields of music, painting, sculpture, or in the field of literature, or in the fields of the nobler drama, but also in that supreme field of oratory,

which in some sense combines the best of all the other
fields, art has a divine right to be; and surely preaching is a form of oratory. And the reason for this is
plain, for art is devoted to a principle with which God
has seen fit everywhere to accompany His proclamation of truth in nature, viz., the principle of beauty.
Art, as well as law, "hath her seat in the bosom of
God."

The prejudice against art in preaching, therefore,
seems to me mistaken and to involve logically an im-
pugning of the very method of God Himself in
dealing with men.

We must retreat upon a far profounder philosophy
of art and of the æsthetic principle in human effort
and in the expression of the human soul.

Let us avoid didactics as much as in us lies, but
remind ourselves of one or two first principles. We
use the word art, I suppose, in two senses:—1st, in
the practical sense, as describing the skillful adaptation of method to gain a given end. In this sense,
oratory is a practical art, because it seeks to persuade
the hearer to practical action.

2d. We employ the word art in the more ideal
sense, to denote the principle which seeks to express a
truth in forms of beauty, with the result of producing
in the mind a certain expansion and delight. This
is the generic use of the word in literature and in the
entire æsthetic realm. Now, the superb glory of the
preacher's art consists in the unique fact that these
two conceptions of art coalesce in their application to
preaching. Preaching is art in the practical sense in
that it is the skillful use of the resources of public

speech to attain the end of practical action. Preaching is art also in the ideal sense in that it seeks to express the highest truth in forms of the purest beauty. But the special point now is that preaching is peculiarly the most noble art in that it unites these two functions, so that the very form and method which fulfill the practical errand, also realize the ideal charm.

In preaching, the really winning is the nobly beautiful, and in no other field of human effort is this identification between the practical and ideal aspects of art so perfect. In our use of the word art, therefore, in the following brief discussion, these two conceptions of art may be merged in one.

Let us then advance by a series of three or four simple steps from the outer and coarser to the inner and finer elements of what we may call art in preaching.

First.—In the outer vestibule of this art stands, of course, the professional technique of the public speaker, the conventional rules for correct and attractive speech, as to the use of the voice, as to manner and gesture. Your text-books tell you these things far better than I could, and they need not detain us now. Here also belong the maxims laid down in the manuals upon rhetoric and logic. Yet important as these rules are they are but the furniture of the vestibule in any true philosophy of art as related to preaching.

Second.—We advance a step further and remind ourselves again of that fundamental principle by which art has everywhere, especially in the noblest ages and among the finest races, enchanted the human mind.   This is, of course, the principle of *beauty*, regarded not as a mere accident of form, not as a mere robe of truth even, but as a part of truth itself, a permanent principle in the Eternal Mind.

May we not surmise even that this mystery of beauty provides the medium between truth on the one hand and joy on the other.   All real sanity includes something of gaiety and grace.   Virgil's sentiment, " Gratior ac pulchro veniens in corpore virtus " is fulfilled in the "grace and truth" of the gospels. The law of art reflects the progress of the mind from truth, through beauty, to joy and joyful action.   Or, to put the matter in another way, beauty bridges the gulf between thought and life.   True art in expression is, therefore, no mannerism, no artifice, but is of the living essence of truth and of man.

The preacher then, as an artist, whether he regards his art on the practical side as a method of winning men or, on the more ideal side, as the incorporation of truth in forms of beauty, should from the beginning cultivate his susceptibility to beauty.   He will discover such beauty in the ordered play of the material world, in man, who is the blossom of the world, in history and in poetry, and in the rhythm of rational thought in the human mind.

One must remind himself, of course, that just here is an easy door into all sorts of foolish fancies.   The candid answer given by his friend to the amateur painter who asked him "about how much do you think I ought to get for this picture?"   "About six months," is not too caustic to apply to the preacher who substitutes high-flown sentiment concerning " ar-

tistic beauty " in the sermon for " the weightier matters of the law, judgment, mercy and faith." But
such fancies are the counterfeit of the real thing we
are speaking of. The preacher must study truth *in*
beauty, and beauty *in* truth.

And this openness of mind to the beautiful may be
cultivated and should be, deliberately and constantly,
—first, in the open air, in fellowship with what St.
Francis would have called his " brothers," the mead-
ows, the rivers and hills, as well as by the open sea
and beneath those " wonderful clear nights of stars,"
to use Stevenson's phrase, which God gives to New
Englanders. It is well that a minister should be
something of a cragsman.

Then, next to this, the young preacher should study
the nobler beauty by reading history and poetry, and
in this order, I think ; that is, if history be read with
something of imagination, and if, on the other hand,
poetry be read with a steady searchlight out for
reality, and perhaps a mental mackintosh ready for
use against gush and bathos, and all that foam of
iridescent fancy-bubbles which look like soaring
spheres, but are exactly " suds " and nothing more.

For because the human mind originates with God,
who always expresses His truth beautifully, therefore
the preacher of God *can* train himself to relish and
adopt something of the method of beauty in stating
God's truth.

And if one is eager to split hairs upon the question
as to the order and rank of precedence in this realm
of the beautiful, he might say this :—that the beauty
of form is higher than the beauty of color, and the

beauty of movement is highest of all. Sinewy, swift logic is beautiful even without a single ornament, as the curve of a cannon shot is beautiful ; and without clear progress there is no beauty in a sermon. Indeed, the very highest beauty is the beauty of moral movement, and this is what we rightly call "grace," the exquisite loveliness of moral action, the quality so characteristic of the "Beautiful Galilean." Thus, as we shall see, the very highest art leads us into the doorway of the Incarnation itself.

What a preacher should strive for is fine form in fit action, and when I say strive, I mean *strive*, as an oarsman trains himself for the race. To use our rifle-shot vernacular, without "go"—and a very fine kind of "go"—there is no sermon. Prolixity, garrulity, which are blemishes in any speaker, are for the preacher sins. Correctness itself is of less value than spontaneity. Who can endure a man so correct that he is nothing else.

Third.—The implement of art for the preacher is *language*. He must train himself, therefore, to honor words. I had almost said to reverence them, because words are more than the mere scenery of thought; they are its "living garment," to employ Goethe's phrase, or, to change the figure, words are precious flasks, brimful of the life of the generations. Philology runs back to biology. "Prose," says Emerson, "is fossil poetry." So it is if we suppose the fossils endued with the cunning art of continuing in life. And we shall further remember that language as such is not only thought in form but thought in beautiful form. The genius of language is the pictorial genius. A word is a picture, a crystal on fire. In the depths of a single, simple word the primary principles of beauty appear, like pearls at the bottom of a pool. It is hardly too much to say, therefore, that a man who would be a true artist in speech, approximates adoration in his sentiment towards language. He takes off his hat in front of a word. He respects language too much to use it carelessly, for in the conception of true art words are the incarnation of spirit.

This divine quality in language is a part of what our brethren who believe in "verbal inspiration" are so unwilling to let slip; and it is well that we should all hold to so much of the doctrine of verbal inspiration as that.

There are, of course, only the commonest fragmentary hints within the arena of this profound and fascinating field, the underlying philosophy of art in public speech. But our errand is specific, and the path is long and we are in haste to arrive at more practical details, so we must hasten onward.

Fourth.—The fourth great principle in the relation of art to preaching appears to be deeper still. It rises into view the moment we remember that the minister is *more* than an orator. He, as a personality, *stands for* his message as well as articulates it. The mere lecturer of the lyceum will enchant his auditors by graceful phrases. The orator of the day at civic celebrations will stir the crowd into what the journals call "billows of enthusiasm." But lecturer and orator pass away. The occasion is an occasion and no more. The man behind the speech, the permanent personality of the orator, is the least emphasized, perhaps the least remembered feature in the performance.

But the preacher on the other hand addresses the same people all the year round. They come to know him. The man behind the speech is the principal thing. Art with him, therefore, the impulse to render the truth in forms of beauty, so as to win mental assent, must relate to other factors besides elocution or even language,—to factors even more intimately personal.

In a word, the law of true art in preaching requires that the preacher shall train *himself* in beauty of soul and of life, so as to be himself a language, an organ of fine expression. The genius of true art is a genius which incarnates. Christian preaching is incarnating the whole soul in words. The preacher must, therefore, develop within himself a certain noble grace of instinctive and habitual feeling and action. He must seek for blended truth and charm in manhood, yet without descending to mannerism, and never losing his first-hand clench on reality. This is why in our profession, as perhaps in no other, character and the steady struggle after character, turn themselves so directly into professional and even literary capital.

We say, therefore, this thing to each other, that we are to seek our best " style," to call it such, in preaching, not in the emphasis upon some one specific literary turn, but in some combination of qualities, which for each man expresses *him*, and nobody else, most and best. The best way to acquire a fine style is to develop a fine soul and then pour out the whole of it in one's preaching. Art, in preaching especially, is, first, to unify manhood, and then to express that unity. Cheap, therefore, is the folly of artificial devices and tricks of declamation. A man should preach as he walks, naturally. Style is the entirety of natural force in free, roused action. Dr. Thompson, master of Trinity College, Cambridge, once thus described a young fop of a tutor—" That all the time he could spare from the adornment of his person he conscientiously devoted to the neglect of his duties." And the satire is not too keen to describe the false method of the young minister who spends his strength in laboriously tying the cravats of rhetoric, studying gesture, now one hand and now the other; who hunts for glittering phrases in quotation marks; who polishes inanities; who in all his utterance suggests the intellectual bandbox and boudoir, *and* forgets the weightier matters of the soul.

Art in preaching then is, after all, chiefly and at the bottom of it, the art of living, making manhood beautiful and holding it so—holding the whole man, clean body, live brain, consecrated spirit,—all as one piece, one lens set in the white light of truth, letting God take care of the image, if only the crystal itself can be kept consistent and clear.

This view of the matter leads directly up, as we shall see in our next lecture, to the consideration of preaching as a genuine and living reincarnation of Christ.

Fifth.—But not to lose ourselves in easy generalization at this point, we can now go on to notice how this principle of true art, the passion for putting truth into beauty for the sake of winning men, pervading not only the literary style of the preacher, but also pervading his intimate life and personality, appears in practical exemplification in the sermon.

According to these principles the sermon is the harmonious synthesis, to speak in pedantic fashion, of three great departments or norms, each of which contributes to it an integral and vital factor.

1st, the subject;

2d, the speaker;

3d, the congregation.

Learning to preach is learning to *tune together* these three factors,—the message given, the man giving it, the man listening to it,—so that in the course of years a certain spontaneous correlation comes to be established between the three, which correlation the preacher incessantly establishes almost without knowing it every time he preaches, and which for him is style.

1st, as to the subject. Is it true, vital, strong, drawn naturally, not only from the text but from the context, and from the entire generic undertone of the document and of scripture at large? Does it carry in it the essential message of the gospel? Have I, the preacher, analyzed it simply, clearly? Have I made the skeleton of it (to use our impertinently anatomical word) symmetrical in articulation,—able to stand on its feet, but with not too many feet? (Two arms also are better than ten, even for a skeleton.) Is the logic of the sermon sound and straight, with pressure cumulative? Are the illustrations brief, pat, not overdone? Have I opened sufficiently, but not wearisomely, the varied wealth of side vistas along the line of thought suggested, without fettering or delaying the mid-march on the main track, until the argument reaches its climax in urgent and kindly appeal ? In a word, is my sermon true to the truth ?

Very well, if it is,—if all these questions are duly answered—then the sermon is just *one-third made.*

2d. The preacher now enters the second field of self-interrogation and asks : " What did God give to *me*, to me myself, in the make-up of my mental faculty ? Is philosophical analysis or imaginative description the faculty that nature put the accent on with me ? Have I put myself, my separate real self, my whole self, into my sermon, in the pattern which I may think God put into the loom for me and meant that I should fill out ? Intellect, humor, pathos, passion, in just my own proper proportion of each, the native hue and rhythm of my mind, have I employed all this in making my sermon ? "

Well, the answer will be, certainly not. Then re-cast the sermon. Rearrange. Rewrite. Drop out all the mere padding from the sermon as it stood at the end of the first scrutiny. Gain space to put in the personal accent,—just as St. Paul did in his letters— the glow of experience, the real individuality of the speaker, so that the sermon, without losing anything that is substantial or vital in the qualities realized under the first norm, is now also clothed with the personal vitality drawn from the second.

Well and good. Your sermon is now *two-thirds* made. But there still remains another third. The preacher now enters a third field of inquiry, retaining, you will observe, what is best of number one and two, but readjusting it to its immediate, practical errand, just as the expert fisherman readjusts his entire theory of fishing and his own habitual method to the particular features of the stream, of the pool, the underbrush, the state of the weather, the exigencies of the hour, the kind of fish he is fishing for at the moment. Questions like these then arise :—My congregation— who are they? What are they thinking about? How do their thoughts go? What do they need? What do they think they need? What order in the succession of ideas (to recall your question No. 42), will most come home to old John Smith down there in the pew, and at the same time strike fire from old John's son just back from college?

The preacher in imagination leaves his pulpit. He becomes each one of a hundred men. He sits in the pew and listens to himself. How queer and sad the resulting impression is! How dull the sermon seems! He perceives that what he has hitherto accomplished in making his sermon is all too subjective. So again out they go from the two-thirds made sermon, all the careless platitudinarian phrases that have crept in under norms one and two, and the man clenches his will and wrings his soul in the determined endeavor to substitute in their place some form of phrase that will *tell* in the brain of these people, even though they are fagged with the week's work. What will arrest? What will move? What will win them? And thus the sermon is again recast. But now, mark! So deep is the reasonableness of true art, so profound the law of true preaching, that the preacher will discover to his astonishment as he undertakes this third task, that nothing really essential to number one and two need be sacrificed for the sake of number three. Then dawns on the young preacher's roused mind the sense of a possible and hitherto undreamed of harmony between these numbers or norms one, two and three, which is for him *style*, a certain rhythm and march of mind in which each department is at its best, and yet all three harmoniously interacting, and in which, as the man grows older and trains himself, they come to interact spontaneously and almost unconsciously.

This is then the way in which the young, really live preacher is willing to drill and discipline himself under his aspiration for noble art in his calling. For the final result is precisely what we have defined noble art to be in this field—the truth of God presented through forms of both personal and literary grace, to the end of securing winning impression upon the mind.

Of these three elements in the sermon it is number three that the young preacher is most apt at first to forget. And yet it is this very number three to which he will give more and more attention as he goes on in his work; for we are all of us at first too subjective.

But there is more in the matter than this. The profounder reason why we come to dwell upon the third class of considerations is that here we feel more and more as we grow older the commanding influence upon true preaching of that deeper and more spiritual conception of it, into which true art at its summit leads us, viz., what I have ventured to call the sense of the genius of the Incarnation. To that great heart of the matter we may try to come next week. Suffice it to say here that it is in this field which sometimes is so pettily called, "adapting oneself to the congregation," that the very innermost spirit of the Incarnation appears. For the spirit of the Incarnation ever "empties itself" as Christ did, is willing to leave its own preferred intellectual palaces even, and while retaining essential truth to itself, will waive something of its selfish luxuries of style, in order to pour itself into moulds of thought, matching with the people yonder, in the burning urgency of its passion to save them.

Not to anticipate, however, and returning to our specific theme to-night, I close with a single reference to that important series of questions which were our starting point in these discussions. The more detailed, practical suggestions in response to them will fall within the compass of the last two lectures of this course, but one general remark may be made here.

You will remember how through those questions, from first to last, runs the peremptory instinct of challenge upon preaching as a practical art, in which three things must be taken into consideration,—the message, the speaker, and the hearer. All the questions relate to one or the other of those three factors. It seemed to be felt by the questioners that preaching must match the present age while losing nothing of its ancestral and sacred distinction. Now this is the very thing we have been speaking of as the object of true art in preaching.

Take question 2, for instance: "What is the message which this age needs?"

Question 27.—"How shall a man sink out of sight

so that men shall feel that they are not spectators of a human performance, but listeners to a divine message ? "

Questions 22 and 24.—" To what extent can the force of personal sympathy be made available in the pulpit ? To what extent should the young preacher use his own experience as a source of illustration ? "

Question 26.—" How shall a man find the common ground between himself and the congregation ? "

Question 31.—" How shall I know, first, the environment, and, secondly, myself in adaptation to it ? "

How straight comes the generic answer to these questions along our path of thought to-night ! So far as Art can answer for Preaching, her answer is, summing up what has been said,—train yourself to *be* in person, and then to express in language truth in forms of grace, Christian truth in forms of Christian grace, for the purpose of winning men, and always to this end put your sermon through three test crucibles, one after the other,—*subject, speaker, hearer—truth, personality, environment,*—in each adding a new element and in each burning all dross away. It is in such vital, trinal synthesis that the preacher finds true success. And in it also he finds power and joy,—in a word, life.

It is a vital necessity that the undertone of preaching should possess this living joy. The preacher must, in the deepest sense of the word, be " *happy* " in his preaching, not thinking about being happy, but really happy, kindled, alert, exhilarated, joyous. With him, as with his Master, the motto is always truth *and* grace. The gospel is good news. Preaching must be genial. You say you are to "preach Calvary." True. And in the holy pathos of its reproduction of the spirit of the Cross lies the power of preaching. But even that Cross stands in the light. It is held up by God's Hand between the gladness of the Nativity and the glory of the Resurrection. "Who for the *joy that was set before Him* endured the cross, despising shame."

The spirit of the true Christian preacher is not that "forlornly brave" altruism, which in our time is the most noble and most pathetic substitute for the gospel, yet with the real gospel left out. The pathos of sympathy, indeed, but also the exhilaration of rescue dwells upon the high terraces to which the genius of Christian art conducts the preacher. His finest art is the product of his truest life, and leads to still higher life.

And thus we find ourselves brought directly in front of that great and holy shrine of our calling, which I have termed *Preaching an Incarnation.*

LECTURE III

PREACHING AN INCARNATION

LECTURE III

PREACHING AN INCARNATION

THE study of preaching as an art brought us into the gateway of that highest thought of preaching which makes of it an incarnation. Or, rather, we found the former aspect of the subject shading up into the latter by insensible though vital gradations.

What then is this higher life of preaching,—the life that pervades it in every part, that distinguishes it in every form, that is the key to its noblest meaning, the law of its most perfect symmetry, the intimate secret of its saving power?

Your own forty-four questions furnish the answer in the conception which we entitle—though the title lies fairly open to criticism as being obscure or as savoring of mysticism—*Preaching an Incarnation.*

Shall we not unite in this simple prayer—May that Master and Lord whom we adore, and to whose reasonable and blessed ministry we have given our strength, aid us to apprehend this inner truth of His calling, as we should, simply, sanely, largely, in rational perspective, without false fancies, but in the clear light of His own holy Word!

Let me allude, in a single sentence to my own experience, and that possibly of many ministers. We spend half a life time in active professional work before we fairly awake to apprehend the truth that preaching is something more than a *report* of the truth, a mere proclamation of the message which historically we know as the gospel.

You will not misapprehend me. We at first conceive of Christ and the body of His doctrine as something historically objective, fixed,—in a sense, statuesque. Preaching is the attempt to call attention to this divine statue, to expound and commend this objective body of truth. But by and by ensues, little by little, a change from this initial conception,—a change so radical that it amounts almost to a new revelation of the way in which Christ's minister may regard his vocation and may cultivate himself with reference to it. And the change is, in a word, this : —the dawning sense, faint at first, but increasing, of the meaning of the truth of the *Incarnation* in its relation to the work of the preacher, especially in this wonderful modern time of ours.

One is easily betrayed into stilted language in speaking of what is a burning verity to his own soul, and yet Emerson's word holds—" Only so much do I know as I have lived." Let me hazard this illustration. It was as though I possessed, in some mental garden, a beautiful statue which I called the gospel, which I had studied a little, looked at from several points of view, walking round and round it, calling attention to its beauties, and expected of course, to find in the morning when I came into the garden, a perfect statue. When, on a sudden, instead of finding my statue, I find a living man, glorious, free, running, racing on the track, with eye on fire and with instant vitality in every limb.

The illustration is clumsy and yet, while the transition of thought of which I am speaking, as to our vocation, is not thus sudden, but gradual and half imperceptible, the greatness of the transition itself is hardly overstated by this fancy of marble becoming man.

But I am certain also that in instants and flashes, at least, this sublimer sense of our calling as a living re-incarnation of our message stirs as if in its sleep in every man of us, from the very beginning of our ministry. If you shall call this latent conception forth and at once throw yourselves out upon it, in Christ's name, you will find your whole vocation, from its very first stadium, transfigured and full of life.

What then do we mean, in the compactest way of putting it, by this phrase—the Genius of the Incarnation, as applied to preaching?

First.—Let us remind ourselves of what the fundamental truth of the Incarnation is, in our irenic Christian faith, for the special idea we are seeking to express is firmly embedded in the central New Testament revelation, as well as supported by the profoundest trend of modern scientific psychology.

Waiving all scholastic refinements, something like this, in a simple, large way of stating it, is our faith; —that the Infinite God, our Father, the supreme, personal Spirit of Life, immanent in the world, as well as transcendent above it, for the sake of men and man's salvation, did pour Himself, in the person of the ineffable and eternal Word, into a selected and most perfect human body and soul, a true and living man, in whom the heart of God thus became manifest

in such wise as would form a living and saving connection with man's world. "The words that I say
unto you, I speak not from myself, but the Father
abiding in me doeth His works" (John 14: 10).
This is the great Incarnation.

And then, beyond this, we believe that this same
supreme law of incarnation, for the sake of spiritual
rescue, still enforced itself and continued to rule in a
second living relation between Christ and those who
were to be His disciples, spokesmen and ambassadors,
which amounted to a kind of secondary incarnation,
though less complete. Nothing short of this is His
own declaration—"I in them and thou in me," an
incarnation of the Incarnation.

Observe the singular radiance of the two converg-
ing lines of light from Christ's words, saying in one
instance, "*I* am the Light of the world," and in another instance, "*Ye* are the light of the world."
"I," "ye." Ye shine by My light in you.

Canon Liddon, in his noble address upon "Our
Lord's Example the Strength of His Ministers,"
speaks of the "imitation of Christ as the regulating
principle of ministerial force." But are we not justified in substituting for that weak word "imitation"
the redder royalty of the word "incarnation"?

Still further, we believe that the agency for this
continued presence of Christ with those who are to
speak for Him is the Holy Spirit; and this Spirit is a
reproducing Spirit. For Who is this Spirit? He is
Christ's Spirit as well as the Spirit of God. "Pro-
ceeding from the Father *and* the Son." The old
intuition, developing itself almost spontaneously in

the more ethical and spiritual Western half of Christendom, finding its first distinct conciliar recognition perhaps at the third council of Toledo, 589, A. D., was justified. It had the genius and the philosophy of the Incarnation behind it.

Listen to Christ's own words, which He is credibly reported to have uttered in the most solemn and tender address which has come down to us in the ancient documents—"When He, the Spirit of Truth, is come, He shall guide you into all the truth." "He shall not speak from Himself." "He shall take of Mine and shall declare it unto you." "He shall teach you all things, and bring to your remembrance all that I said unto you." That is to say, the Holy Spirit *carries on* the life of Christ in the soul under the law of a continued and spiritualized incarnation. To this agrees that profound and powerful phrase of St. Paul— "The law of the spirit of life in Christ Jesus." This is the law of the incarnation, and is a permanently acting law. "No *chrisma* without *charisma*," says Christlieb.

Now you will reply, and it is perfectly true, that this principle of the living Christ with men and within men is not the solitary prerogative of the Christian minister; it is at the heart of all true Christian manhood as well. Certainly. And just because it is, it preeminently constitutes the glowing heart of the minister's special work, which is nothing unless it springs aloft from the ground floor of a full Christian manhood. "Lay" preachers are often real preachers.

Second.—We go on then a step further and inquire how this general principle of Christian incarnation relates itself to preaching. It plainly represents itself under two aspects.—The one aspect is that wherein we may conceive such a derivative and secondary incarnation promoted through *our own volition;* that is, it is the man himself seeking to embody Christ's Spirit and Truth. The other aspect is that of an incarnation accomplished through *Christ's volition in us,* using the natural force of the man as His own organ of expression. Though practically blended in consciousness and work, these two aspects of the idea of incarnation may be theoretically discriminated for the sake of clearness in thought.

In the former of these two fields a preacher may strive to incarnate Christ's truth in this sense, that by a strenuous self-discipline he *is training himself* to reproduce, not only by spoken word but by his whole attitude of manhood, by his feeling and action in preaching, the spiritual tone and message of his Master. This is the "Holy Place" of the incarnation. The volitional energy is the man's own. Here appears the necessity for that full-toned manhood which is the true ministerial manhood. The minister takes account of his entire self—his "one world" to use Herbert's phrase,—his body, brain, sensibility, as well as the great central fires of spiritual impulse, as an organ of expression which *he* himself is to train and fill with the reproduced thought and spirit of Christ and His revelation.

But beyond this is there not still a more sacred and interior phase of the matter? "Let each man think himself an act of God."[1] The minister, cleaving to his New Testament, may humbly dare to regard him-

[1] "Festus," Bailey.

self thus disciplined, as an instrument which Christ Himself may deign to touch and use in the mystery of His life and grace. This surely is the "Holy of Holies" of the preacher's "incarnation,"—a realm of the mind, where *Christ's* personal, living power may be supposed to supply the initial impulse, the inspiration. "It is no longer I that live but Christ liveth in me." May not the wonderful utterance fit in with any man or minister as truly as with St. Paul?

In the practical consciousness of the preacher however, these two mental processes, which we have called the "Holy Place" and the "Holy of Holies," are not separated. Perhaps we cannot separate them or draw a line where one ends and the other begins, for as to this very innermost mystery, to what extent Christ our Master will choose to use us, to come in and dwell with us and speak through us in this regard, we cannot dare to say. In a sense, we have nothing to do with it. It is Christ's matter. It is here that a sane man would be most upon his guard against subtle forms of pride, of extravagance, of esoteric fancy. What we do need is to train ourselves in the outer of these arenas. Then when *He will* He can find us fit, or let us say a little less unfit, to His hand.

It will perhaps be difficult to avoid the impression that, speaking in this way, we have in mind something novel, far-fetched, perhaps fantastic or unscriptural, and no doubt, as must be again emphasized, the door opens here readily enough to all sorts of mawkish conceits and foolish fancies, which are the counterfeits of the real scriptural thing we have in mind. But these counterfeits are all of them distinguished by lack of two things—symmetry and scriptural warrant—as well as by the lack of two other accompanying qualities, which are, I think, the two salts of the soul,—humor and humility.

Third.—What then, more particularly, is the relation of this reincarnating principle to the preacher's individuality and personal independence? And the answer is perfectly plain, though, as Pascal remarks in another connection—"We feel it better than we can express it." Christ's living Spirit surely respects the free personality of His minister, not substituting Himself for us, nor in any way suppressing our own individuality nor discarding its limitations. Indeed, that is not the genius of incarnation at all. The true genius of incarnation honors and even exalts the individuality of the form it chooses. From the depths of the universal Christian faith emerges this clear logic, that even as the Eternal God respected the true manhood of Christ Jesus, the Son of Mary, and conformed Himself to the human Jesus in the mystery of the Great Incarnation, so now, also, the Spirit of Christ does honor to the mystery of free human personality, recognizes its independence, and the application to it of the natural laws of mind, while yet employing this complex product of free power and natural law as a mould, a living body, into which something of His continued life may, through His grace, flow.

It seems necessary to emphasize this strongly, and bolt the door against easy misconception at this vital point, for if any one supposes that the endeavor to preach in the light of this truth, in the noble effort to reembody as well as to report the gospel will result in the suppression of virile independence, will make preachers echoes merely of the past, amiable dreamers, acolytes of a mystic cult, lifted up with a subtle spiritual pride instead of manly, secular, up-to-date men, he has mistaken the very idea of incarnation; for the incarnation of God *in* man is not the substitution of God *for* man. Incarnation " comes forth into the light of things," to use Wordsworth's fine phrase, and maintains the integrity of the personal form into which the incarnation is made.

And this also must be borne in mind, that true incarnation is an incarnation into the whole of a man's manhood, not into a segment of it. The kingdom of God in man's soul, or in the preacher's vocation, knows no fractional psychology. God will not discredit the stamp He first put upon an individual man by any subsequent use He makes of him. How curious it is that Peter and John were less like each other, and yet were each of them more like Christ at the end of their three years' companionship with Him than at the beginning ? The soldier whistle of that initial *S* was not quite lost in the *P* when Saul became Paul. And the time would fail me to tell of Justin and Jerome and Chrysostom and Columba far in the West, and Savonarola and Luther and Knox, who, each and all, reembodying the one spirit of their Master, found also the separate individuality of each mind called into distinctive action in the form suited to its own environment and time.

This scriptural truth of preaching then, as being in some sense a reincarnation of Christ in the roused and refined manhood and utterance of the preacher,

does not take a man one inch away from actual
people and practical life, but, on the contrary, brings
us nearer to them.   It is an idea not esoteric or even
mystical, save in the healthy, legitimate sense of that
word.   It does not substitute an inner illumination
for the plain, sane sense of things.   It is simply the
practical realization in the field of the ministry of
what we Christians all say we believe as to the divine
element in human life and form.   The form *must* be
human, natural, red-blooded, else that word incarnation
with the wonderful glow of live color in its depths does
not apply.

All that "piece of work" which constitutes the
man, the personal feature and faculty, the native
rhythm and march of mind, its free energy, humor,
gaiety and practical sympathy, the whole full-toned
orchestra of the human power, "the primordial mass
of manhood," as Dr. Stalker calls it, is not, in the
least, disowned or set aside for something occult,
rarified and ethereal.   This is substitution, not incarnation.

You cannot, my comrades, feel half so keenly as I
feel, how pallid and barren these words are to suggest
even the content of this great and manly truth we are
invoking.   The idea itself is really the "eternal song"
of our great vocation; but it is a "song without
words" or rather beyond them.   One cannot seem to
put into words what is tugging and struggling in his
heart to be said, in front of this wonderful shrine of
our calling.

But I pray God that this plain inadequacy on my
part may only stir you up to articulate these things for

yourselves, for you can do this, and to listen to the deeper voice of your own souls. And this would be best of all. For we shall discover that our current phrases about "bringing Christ" into our ministry, are not "vain imaginings," the ghosts of forgotten speculations, but they denote palpitating realities, such as send a living thrill through all the body and soul of a man, stirring him to his finger-tips, reaching to the most hidden cranny of his mind, kindling his intense and chivalrous passion, not only to secure that "beauty of the inward soul" for which Socrates prays, at the close of the "Phaedrus," but also to make himself, even to the last filament of his manhood, a white, true organ of expression, in touch with Christ and His truth on the one hand, and with our living age on the other, so that without impairing the play and power of free personality, something of the very power of Christ may also, perchance, rest upon him.

Fourth.—But not to lose ourselves in generalities, hugging the practical and aiming straight at our target, let us, in the fourth place, go still one step further along the same road. For as you have observed, we have already come within the border of a still further extension of the law of the incarnation, as applied to preaching. It is this:—Not only does the preacher seek incessantly to unify and train himself properly to embody as well as to report Christ's truth, he also in turn creates a new form, selected from the best of the life of the age he lives in and the mental habit of the people whom he addresses ; and into that new form, suited to the people, he pours his sense of the ancient truth, so that it shall come to the people in the phrase of the people.

The fine thing here must be touched half gaily, else it will be touched mawkishly. For one fancies that precisely here is where the subtlest self-sacrifice of the preacher flashes at the finial into his finest power. Here is the preacher's cross, but also his crown. For you of course perceive how often at this point the preacher must "cease from himself," set aside his own selfishly preferred form of expression and choose one caught up from the people. Without this our spiritual intensities may go over the heads of actual men, and even seem to remove us from them. One can imagine himself growing so flamingly intense and lifted up as to lose humor and proportion, and so really to lessen actual fellowship with what in its cooler mood the congregation is thinking about and feeling. A preacher may be so keyed up and spiritually exalted that without knowing it he becomes unpractical, unnatural, ungenial, stilted, overstrained. Through all this plays also a kind of latent spiritual pride.

The corrective against this subtle peril of high spiritual passion is to realize the true genius of the incarnation by which, with a certain profound and delicate spiritual self-denial, the man comes down from his high places, takes the distilled essence of his own spiritual excitement, and pours it into the flasks of every-day, commonplace sympathies and expressions derived from the people.

But you will also perceive that the law of incarnation requires the preacher to select for this purpose the *best* forms of the people's life and thought. He must pick out the choicest factors of the new time, the finest habits of mental movement, the kindliest sympathies germane to the people in front of him. These he must combine, and in that finest selection from the environment he must express his thought and, as we have seen, endeavor to reincarnate, as God may give him grace, the "truth as it was in Jesus."

And so we come in sight of the entire scheme and march of the student's thought upon this subject, how the philosophy of noble art in preaching shades up, or rather brightens up, into the philosophy of the incarnation itself, and how this in turn leads us straight on to employ what is truest and newest in our modern time. This will be our special theme in the following lecture.

O my associates, is it not a thrilling thing to preach, or even to try to preach and fail, in the glory of such an idea of preaching as this, with Christ behind us, so near that He can touch us, and with the living men of to-day in front of us, so near that we can touch them !

I recall one very remarkable sentence of Scripture which has come down to us in one of the great un-contested Epistles of St. Paul, the second to the Corinthians, which in an almost startling fashion pre-sents both wings of this dual process. The sentence is this:—"For we preach not ourselves but Christ Jesus, as Lord." This is the first half of the sentence. Here is presented the notion of the incarnation of Christ's spirit in the form of the personal effort and energy of the minister. Now read on—"And ourselves as your servants, for Jesus' sake "—the minister's reembodiment of this same spirit in the dialect of the people, for that is the undertone of the idea. In a superficial sense Paul contradicts himself : in a deeper sense he does not. In one breath Paul declares that we do *not* preach ourselves, and yet *do* preach ourselves ; but it is only as " servants " of the people, and yet Christ is in all the process—" for Jesus' sake."

Midway, then, we stand,—God help us to stand there humbly and largely—between Christ and the people, between the white shrine and the leaping flame, true to the one, fair to the other, while the law of the incarnation, " the spirit of life in Christ Jesus," pervades all, first from Christ to His minister, then from that minister to men.

" The dignity of truth," as old Ben Jonson said, " is lost with much protesting." And we rein ourselves back from overstatement, but we cannot help feeling that here is unrolled before us the magnificent rationality and breadth of the true conception of preaching.

It is this dual harmony in ministerial culture, which we are perhaps in danger of missing the true authority for, which constitutes the peculiar enthusiasm of our calling. In the one direction we " see Jesus." With the mind's eye, illuminated still further by Christ's Holy Spirit of promise, again we behold that dear Syrian face. His voice again is on the air, His touch is on our souls, His truth seeks reembodiment in all our manhood ; while, on the other hand, all that we have within us that is nimblest, bravest, most intelligent rushes forth into the new age, to understand it, to grasp it, to affiliate with the best in it, to make it a new shrine of Christ, a new temple of God. The whole battalion of the time is thus marching for us preachers. All its splendid and varied materials, its surpassing jets of power, crowd up to our hand, to be utilized and in a sense incorporated in our work. What a thing it is to be a preacher to-day !

Fifth, and finally.—We are led by this line of discussion, in which generals rather than particulars have been considered, (with the result of making the lecture explicitly monotonous, but that you must please forgive) directly to three groups of practical inferences.

1st. A new and commanding accent falls upon the minister's self-culture ; for what stirs him is the new idea of cultivating not his ministerial self alone, but his whole self to be his ministerial self, in the humble effort to become, so far as God will, Christ's organ of speech to living men.

Now the power of this thought is that it immensely enlarges the range of resources which one is impelled to use in preaching. It induces what is more important than anything else for the preacher,—a certain constant energy and exhilaration in his way of thinking and acting, in reference to his work. With his one great end in view, he will make of his body, for example, the finest and most facile body possible. Of course he cannot, unless he be a man of more than average stature, produce the impression which Sidney Smith said that Daniel Webster made upon him—that the great American was "a locomotive in trousers,"—but he can insist with himself that his body shall take the accent of the gentleman in all personal niceties, and he will drill and hammer that body until it obeys him. He will not allow his casual mood to have its way. He will drive with a tight rein. He can and he will deny himself those trivial personal indulgences which dissipate energy and weaken will. And he will remember what the accomplished President of Dartmouth put so aptly in his Yale Lectures on Preaching, that for the preacher "the subtle refinement of laziness is the postponement of the hard and exacting duty beyond the one which is easier and more agreeable." He will smite at all "blue devils." He will keep himself strung and sunny. He will "down" all petulance, throttle all jealousy. He will laugh cynicism out of court. He will even refrain from gossip "as much as lieth in him." He will ridicule himself out of his own self-conceit, avoid flippancy, and especially watch and guard against that negligence in spare hours which so easily ravels down into acrid or effeminate or apathetic or gloomy tempers.

Then, in the realm of the intellect. He will not be contented with the French *mot*, that "the fragments of the intellect are always good." [1] He will cultivate especially that generic intellectual habit, wherein is justice, breadth, swift movement. He will train his mind to think of things in Christ's way. He will endeavor to realize in his own intellectual life Christ's way of regarding God, the world, the soul.

Then, deepest of all, in the realm of the spirit, he

[1] "Handsome Lawrence," George Sand.

will strive with a great striving that he may winnow his soul free of what would obstruct the natural play through him of the mind of his Lord, and, at the same time, he opens every window into the actual life of men around him. For the sake of others, he "sanctifies himself" as his Master did, so that at the end of years and years of this symmetrical self-disciplining of body, brain, and spirit, all together and all in one, he can find himself one glowing unit of force, not all unready for the Master's hand.

Now, it is nothing less than marvellous how this personal training transforms itself into a professional power as far from self-conceit as it is from cowardice. In default of special talent even, a man who fills himself with these splendid ideals as to the relation of personal manhood to preaching, and maintains himself in this attitude of the inner spirit, will, at length, come to surpass, in all the higher efficiency of his work, the man who possesses talent with less of moral enthusiasm, for back of the former of the two men is the very Genius of the Incarnation, inspiring and supporting him.

2d. Then a second practical inference from our general line of thought also follows. We find ourselves in a new and advantageous position with regard to the critical discussions of the hour. The "Higher Criticism" is best studied from above, from the table-lands of spiritual aspiration. We retain that larger perspective of thought and of faith which the detail of current criticism is under some risk of losing. Brethren, some things are not of so much consequence as other things are, an axiom which might be written upon the door of the minister's study and even possibly in theological halls.

No mistake, however, is more serious than to belittle current discussion, for in our age also, as truly as in any former age, the Spirit of God is moving, and is moving through the agency of this very discussion and criticism itself.

Yet, when we put the preacher's work into these large categories which we have ventured to entitle those of art and incarnation, we are introduced, I am sure, into a region above and beyond many of the critical cleavages. The effort to embody in the forms of a finished and noble art something of the spirit of Christ, for the sake of the rescue of men and the spiritual enfranchisement of modern society, is an errand so large that a preacher finds himself in practical sympathy with what is good on both sides of cotemporary controversy. He sees the seamless overarch of the one sky above "conservative" and "liberal." He feels the granite continuity of the one world beneath the level to which the cleavage runs, and therefore he is Christ's freeman, and every man's brother in the tossing time. Not that he will be a trimmer, or a neutral. He will have clear convictions, decided opinions perhaps on points of issue; but no man can tether him or label him as a partisan. His preaching will somehow make men feel that the important things are both nearer and surer than the points of controversy.

And more than this. In this swift march the preacher finds himself in the way of the practical settlement for himself of many vexed questions which are baffling, perhaps paralyzing, so long as he sits alone in the chill of the merely critical mood. It is easy to find that cold chair of hesitant intellectual misgiving. Quit it.

We *work* ourselves out of intellectual perplexity by working up into the larger vision that commands both sides of mooted questions, as the cragsman emerges from valley mists while he climbs to the sunny terraces of the upper mountains. The endeavor to reembody the old message in the new time gives to the preacher a new principle of discrimination, a new secret of reconciliation and adjustment, and he gains, both for himself and for his people, new insight, new freedom, new mastery in all the critical field.

3d. Then, third and last of these practical conclusions, we discover an answer to certain of your forty-four questions. "Thou sayest an undisputed thing in such a solemn way," said our genial Dr. Holmes, I suspect with a shrewd eye to us ministers. Accordingly, your salvation, gentlemen, from the didactic monotone of these lectures, is in your own straight rifle-shot questions. How swiftly they ride ahead of us along our track! Some of these questions however are simply unanswerable if we remain on the lower professional levels, but on this higher level of realizing what the genius of the incarnation is, as related to our vocation, we attain a certain point of vantage, a certain kindled glow of mind and life, in which the questions answer themselves.

Take that tremendous question, for example, number 32—"What are the certainties of truth which will be most effective with a congregation?" What a question that is! How every man of us feels the instant weight of it! You know the conventional current answer. It is that the "Christological" order of truth is the most effective in preaching. Yet this answer seems somehow tame and theoretic. But our point of view to-day gives us a different conception of the whole matter, for the Christological order, what is it? It is not the mere common idea of preaching chiefly about Christ. That is part of it. But the Christological order is the order of divine truth *as it lay in Christ's mind.* That translated into the preacher's mind and again retranslated by him into the mental dialect of the people of the time, is the effective order. Preach most what Christ thought about most, what He makes you think about most, what you can make people think about most— those three in one. Preach God in Christ's way. Preach moral ideals with Christ's accent. It is this *cadence of Christ* which is the effective thing—this exquisite rational grace in the *tone* of the Sermon on the Mount, for example, or in those final syllables in the "upper room."

Or, take that other question, number 36, only second in importance—"What are the qualities to rate highest in taking inventory of our own resources?" And the answer is equally direct and unconventional. Those qualities are best that best take the stamp of the incarnating principle in its dual operation. Those qualities of mind and heart stand first for a preacher which most readily apprehend and affiliate with Christ

on the one hand, and with humanity on the other.
We should cultivate, for example, that side of the intellect which lies towards sympathy, that side of the
imagination that lies towards reverence, that side of
the orator's passion which lies towards sincerity, simplicity, humility.

And then question 25—"Shall one put personal
experience into sermonic form?" Yes, certainly, but
not in the crude, conceited way of turning autobiog-
rapher every Sunday. Few ministers can stand that,
and still fewer congregations can. It is apt to beget
a certain coolness—a "glacial epoch"—between pulpit and pew. The true way to use one's own personal
experience is as an interpreter between Christ's truth
and the *people's* experience. People are more interested in their own experience than in yours. We
really are most finely using ourselves when we "cease
from ourselves." Perhaps on the larger scale we are
never more really "succeeding," or being more truly
aided by the "Spirit of Truth and of Grace" than
when we are seeming to ourselves more than half to
"fail."

Thus also question 26 is answered—"How can a
man find the common ground between himself and the
congregation?" The answer is—by rising to a new
and higher level. If the preacher is "alive" in the
sense we have tried to define, then the essential human
truth and tone of Christ, caught up by the preacher,
is so reproduced through him as to reach the answering chord in the people. The high ground is the
common ground.

Last of all, our principle corresponds with that

strong note in question 27. I can imagine the deep place in the writer's mind out of which that question came. "How shall a man sink out of sight so that men shall feel that they are not spectators of a human performance, but listeners to a divine message?"

In an obtrusive or self-seeking sense, the preacher does "sink out of sight." But he does not try to sink. There is no unmanly gasp of mechanical self-abasement. He is hurrying with Christ's torch to men's dark homes, and he is too eager about the torch to think or to care what his own pose is. Striving so far as his uttermost faculty may to reembody the spirit of his Lord, and on the other hand setting aside his own mere fancies of style and pouring his very soul into the flasks of form furnished by the best mental habit of the people in front of him and of the age around him, he does efface himself, but it is by making himself the finest possible man, as the perfect lens itself is not seen through which the eye looks at the star.

The man is thus protected against many of the worst dangers of our calling, which have been the sources of weakness to the ministry and discredit to the Church. He is protected against mawkishness, against fanaticism, against vainglory and spiritual pride, against barren scholasticism, against demagognism under the mask of evangelistic zeal, against esoteric pietism. On the contrary, he is reasonable, sympathetic, true, a good fellow, a sensible, healthy comrade. He is of the people, as his Master was. But within it all, he is a *man on fire* with the unmatched passion of his great calling, from which sprang the old, fervid words, so long ago written down by a master hand—"As though God *were entreating by us*. We beseech you on behalf of Christ, be ye reconciled to God."

THE NEW AGE AND ITS RELATION TO
PREACHING

LECTURE IV

THE NEW AGE AND ITS RELATION TO PREACHING

NOTHING could be further from the simple path of inquiry purposed in these lectures, than to enter upon the endeavor to describe and analyze at length the significant factors and forces of our "New Age," as we not incorrectly term it. Your own minds, as disclosed in your forty-four questions, are themselves products of this new age, and are alive to its characteristic note.

Our one object now is to ask how the line of argument thus far pursued relates itself to this characteristic note of the modern time. That line of argument briefly recalled is as follows:

Preaching is first a noble art of public speech, by which, setting forth Christian truth in gracious forms, the preacher brings his subject, himself and his congregation into moral harmony, and so wins the mind. But beyond this, preaching is also an incarnation, and nothing short of that, a reincarnation, under human limitations, of the "Mind of Christ"—a reembodiment, to some extent, of the Spirit of the Great Incarnation in Christ Jesus, in which art, though still present, ceases to be self-conscious, and in which the preacher, with every kindled faculty, seeks to train his manhood in its entirety into one finished organ of expression, so as to represent, as well as to report,

79

something of the message of his Master, and so that even possibly that Master Himself, in the mystery of His living presence, shall find His servant not unready to His use, as the humble exponent of His Spirit speaking to men.

But the logic of all this leads the preacher still further, namely, into the incessant and resolute endeavor to select from the finest factors of the present age, and the noblest mental habit of the men whom he addresses, a yet fresher form or mould of incarnating expression, a model of utterance, a manner of action, best suited to men to-day, into which, without loss, he may pour the vital essence of the ancient truth.

The natural and easy criticism upon all this line of thought is, of course, that it is mystical and runs off into mere transcendentalism ; and it may be acknowledged that our path does lie along close to such a gulf of misty vagaries, from which the true idea must be carefully discriminated.

But we have now reached a point in the discussion where the general conception of preaching which we have sought to develop and which pervades your initial questions, can be put to final and practical test. If that conception fails to stand the fire of actual demand to-day, if it fails to connect itself, readily, naturally, vitally, with the specific practical problems of the modern age, it must be set aside.

I believe, however, that this modern note involves no substantial change in our point of view or our line of reasoning, namely, that which regards preaching as a practical art, leading up into a spiritual incarnation.

On the contrary, at this very point such a conception most evinces its rational practicality and spiritual power.

This brings us then, in thought, fairly within the gates of the new age, in the midst of an arena as bewildering as it is stimulating, and we ask, with a sort of excited misgiving, how can we carry out any such lofty ideal of our calling amid the toss and rush of the modern era? What are these factors which the minister can choose and use from the time and in the time and for the time? What sentiments in our age are best for the minister to single out, correlate and combine into a new instrument of form through which the law and genius of the Incarnation bid him speak?

May I mention briefly four of these factors, which are perhaps of chief importance to the preacher? They are those which lie plainest upon the face of things, involving no recondite analysis in order to discern them; and they are those which your own questions emphasize.

Question No. 28, for example—"Can you give us a relief picture of the arena in which we are to have our task?"

No. 29—"What I want is something objective, a clear analysis of the conditions of society?"

No. 39—"What I want is knowledge of the field from a man who has been there," (and escaped alive! —though you did not say that).

The four features of our time most important for present consideration appear to be: —

1. The spirit of scientific investigation and criticism;

2.   The spirit of social combination;

3.   The spirit of economic enterprise;

4.   The spirit of the new philanthropy, by which I mean the philanthropy which seeks to deal intelligently with causes of misery, as well as with misery itself.

These four, if I mistake not, are vitally inter-related, leading up one from another, like a terrace with four steps.

I shall not quarrel, of course, with the man who affirms that on each of these four levels we find ourselves confronted by an intellectual medley—" an orgie of thought," to recall a phrase of Amiel written thirty years ago,—an imposing but heterogeneous mixture of good and evil elements; but I maintain that the central idea in each of these four modern movements is of God, and offers itself most nobly to the preacher's hand.

> " This world's no blot for us,
>   Nor blank; it means intensity and means good."

1st.—Take, first, if you please, our uncompromising friend, the spirit of scientific criticism. I need not delay upon any labored restatement of this modern temper. It is the breath of all our breathing. Our object at the moment is simply to ask, how shall the true preacher of Christ who, in the spirit of a noble art, seeks also to reincarnate the gospel message in the finest forms of the current age, adjust his preaching to the demands of this critical spirit? In the field of Biblical criticism, for example, where shall he set up his pulpit? The answer which our logic gives us is perfectly plain. The true scientific temper is essentially rational and right. It is of God and leads to God. The preacher, therefore, should keep himself in sympathy with the generic spirit of modern criticism, while holding at easy arm's length certain alleged results of that criticism. Criticism is "Higher" if it leads us higher. Critical verdicts are, many of them, tentative, and preaching should not often be tentative. Nor do these verdicts change the heart of the gospel; and preaching must always be of the heart of the gospel. But on the other hand, the believer in God and in His "firm path through the stream of ages" must dare to take distinctly this point of view, even in the pulpit, namely, that the great critical movement in modern thought reveals the breathing of the Spirit of God upon the intellect of man and is to be rejoiced in and honored. Criticism is a phase of faith.

The accomplished author of "The Gospel for an Age of Doubt" will forgive our query, whether even more than an "age of doubt" this age be not one of struggle against doubt in the interest of the finer faith and the nobler spirituality. Not alien from our time is the Spirit of Him who said,—"Ye shall know the truth and the truth shall make you free."

The spirit of this age never stops with doubt. It is impatient with doubt. It hurries to its lens and its drill that it may dispel doubt and supplant misgiving by certainty. Critical investigation is a mark not of doubt but of faith, *in battle*. It is "the removing of those things that are shaken, as of things that have been made, *that*" (the force of the sentence is in the conjunction) " those things which are not shaken may remain." An age of power can never be predominantly an age of doubt.

The intellectual undertone of our time is not that of relish for doubt, but that of hunger for truth, and this hunger is of God.

The long misunderstood, foolishly discredited doctrine of "evolution," for example, to use the current general title, as describing one of the methods of the divine operation, is logically the parent of the new conservatism, as well as of the new criticism. It agrees with true Theism in its doctrine of the immanence of God in the process of human history and the development of the human mind, and it agrees also with that more special Christian doctrine of the continued spiritual presence of Christ with His true Church,—a doctrine with the renaissance of which the new century is opening and which is now the enthusiasm of many Christian souls. We are living in the restoration of the Christological perspective, and criticism is contributing to this restoration.

Any sane preacher will be on his guard here, of course, to avoid that vague and hazy half materialistic pantheism which is the subtle counterfeit of the thing we are talking about. But we shall not be so afraid of counterfeits as to refuse true gold.

Christian scholarship rejoices in the deepening certainty that the philosophy of evolution contains a true apprehension of one way of the divine working, and that rightly stated it is, so far as it goes, the strongest intellectual ally yet discovered to the early spiritual intuitions of Christian faith. It proclaims the survival of the fittest, and, therefore, turning the argument around, the fitness of that, which, after the testing of fair fight, survives, is so far forth demonstrated. According to this, real orthodoxy can never become obsolete, but is always rational. Reason and faith join hands to proclaim that the God of the old times is the God of the new times ; that if Christ's Spirit was immanent in the Church as a living power in the first century or the fourth or the sixteenth, it is not less immanent in the Christendom of the twentieth—that the social movements and tumults of to-day are the very waves upon which the Master's feet come walking.

This is a familiar note in these halls. Surely without any approach to what might seem cheap in compliment or invidious in comparison, I may express the common debt of Christian scholarship, and especially of our Congregational churches, to this institution and to its honored President, for the distinct and fearless proclamation of the living truth that modern Sociology is in large measure Christology in the application ; that the laws of social evolution are laws of the advancing Kingdom of our Lord Jesus Christ.

New discoveries, ideals, achievements are more old than they are new. They are fresh phases of one continuing Divine Kingdom. There is no " listless ripple of oblivion," to echo Stephen Phillips' over-labored " Greek phrase," and " Christ " is not " in Hades." The special rhythm of mental life is new, but in it—in the present union of a critical intellectual temper with a devoted altruism, we are to find not only the mark of Christ upon the age, but a kind of resurrection of Christ Himself,—His sweet sanity, His "grace and truth."

Now let us apply this. Take that group of our questions, numbers 7, 8, 9 and 10, concerning the preacher's discussion of Higher Criticism. Shall he seek such discussion or shun it? Neither, for the most part. But when he does speak, let the discussion be both fearless and fair. Let the final impression be always one of intellectual justice, mingled with unshaken faith. The desirable thing is critical insight, together with spiritual enthusiasm. A sermon should never close leaving the weight of emphasis on the doubt.

Suppose, preaching from Isaiah, the preacher occupies the first third of a given sermon with a fair, large, non-technical, non-partisan account of the question as to the composite authorship of the great book. But if, then, during the remaining two-thirds of that sermon he makes the moments weighty with the moral and religious truths which God has revealed on those stately pages, whether by one or by all the Isaiahs, what will the people say? They will say, 'That is right ; that strikes the true chord ; that gives the true intellectual and moral perspective. Such preaching presents the old time and the new time together, the old truth in the reincarnation of the current age.'

What is the preacher's twentieth century? It is the whole age just as it is, but *including Christ.* Precisely as Christianity illustrated its intellectual and cosmopolitan genius by adopting the Greek language in the early centuries as its fit and facile organ of expression, so now the same Christianity adopts the scientific spirit, which is the Greek language of the modern time, as the equally appropriate channel for its expression to-day.

Science leads us to Nature, and Nature leads us to the Son of Mary, and then stands silent. Jesus said, "Consider the lilies," and science obeys Him. The finest spirit of science is profoundly in harmony with the spirit of Christianity as disclosing in human form an incarnation of God.

Debate is necessary ; it always has been necessary. The history of doctrine attests the survival of the fittest through antagonism in the realm of thought. The best statements of Christian truth have always been evolved through free and often fiery discussion. "I come not to send peace" but an intellectual "sword," is the spirit of Christ's maxim ;—but at bottom, the preacher's truth is this, that it is the Life of God, the Spirit of Christ, which, working through the human intellect, in subtle and spiritual ways, is bringing in these present critical changes, by which the spirit of formalism is swept aside, and the spirit of traditionalism supplanted by the spirit of rational inquiry, of intellectual humility, and of a deepened spirituality.

2d. The rigid limitations of time which courtesy must impose upon these lectures, forbid more than the barest allusion to the other three characteristic forces in our age which the preacher may, in similar manner, seize upon and utilize in order to fashion his "mold of form" suited to men to-day.

Next after the spirit of scientific investigation and criticism comes the spirit of social combination.

This is largely the product of the scientific study of the history of man. Sociology is science applied to social life.

It is a platitude now to assert that perhaps the most vital phenomenon of the last quarter of the nineteenth century is the new sense of society as a corporate human unity, with its own laws of growth. As you know, an entire new literature has sprung into existence upon this field. New departments have been opened in every college, and new chairs established. What have we as Christian ministers to say of this astonishing new disclosure of social laws, of social possibilities? We have distinctly to say this, that while many of the modern developments in this field are crude, many false, some obnoxious and perilous to the State, yet beneath all else is a genuine renaissance of Christ's Christianity. You will not misunderstand. The field of "sociology" is wild with warring and stormy voices, but the "deeper voice across the storm" is calling back and on and up to Christ. I must think that if Christ were to speak now He would surprise us all by how much in the modern world He would approve. During nineteen centuries His Spirit has been at work, and He would not disavow the results of that working. He *is* "standing at this latter day upon the earth." We must detect His smile on the time.

What a fact, and what a force exists, then, here at hand for the preacher, not only for him to perceive and honor, but adopt and incorporate as to its spirit in his own method and style of utterance. So will he reach the people; so will he obey the law of incarnation. He will reproduce Christ's fellow-feeling with the people. Christian sociology should reappear in the preacher in the form of Christian geniality.

This is a very different thing, and a much subtler and more spiritual thing than preaching about "social questions" and "burning questions," etc. The preacher "preaches Christ" always, but preaches Him in the dialect furnished by the forms in which Christ's own Spirit is working in the age. We need not preach "sociology" in the technical sense, but we must apprehend, to use Ezekiel's burning symbol —"The spirit of live" within the modern "wheels," and make evident to the people Christ's own accent on it, and in it.

One must of course apologize in front of these colossal modern movements for an allusion to them so fragmentary and meagre. But there is no other option in these brief addresses. Suffice it to say further at this point, that such sympathy with the modern social spirit is the only source of practical answer to certain of your own questions.

Here is question No. 20, for example —

"How are young men to be led to the Church?"

No. 21—"How to reach the children?"

These questions cannot be answered by mechanism, by devices, by patent prescriptions. The preacher who would attain these ends by mere rules will fail. He is to attain them by bringing his manhood and his preaching into a certain tone of vivid sympathy with Christ on the one hand, and the social life of the time on the other. At whatever cost to himself, let him come down from his antiquated or factitious professional pedestals, and stand with Christ and childhood on the bright floor of the new age.

3d. The third modern force which offers itself to the preacher is the Spirit of Industrial Enterprise. And what is this? Is it not at heart the union of the scientific spirit with the social spirit in application to practical life? And how shall the preacher, therefore, regard this modern industrial realm? As a field remote from if not alien to his own? Not if he is wise. Here also the undertone of the current age is of the very essence of the Kingdom of God. Here in this secular field also is an unsuspected disclosure of both a poetry and a religion. The accuracy, alertness, fidelity, insisted on in modern industrial life, is in the line of ethical discipline. The "signal-station" man must have a conscience, and the age tends to make every man a "signal-station" man. Rudyard Kipling, whose curious and athletic "break" into literature, however at the moment perhaps discredited, is one of the signs of the times, has opened to us somewhat of the unthought-of poetry of industrialism. On how far finer and deeper scale is there not also a Christology of industrialism !

But how shall the preacher incorporate and utilize the industrial spirit? By talking about "industrials"? Men would laugh at him. The preacher's art is more spiritual than that. "The message which God sends is spiritual," says Bishop Simpson. The preacher should embody in his sermon a certain tone, caught up from the industrial life about him, a habit of practicality, of swift and sinewy movement in style, of Saxon brevity instead of Latin rotundity, of concrete wrestle with actual fact, a tone which the business man appreciates without knowing why he likes it.

In our age the preacher has no business to stand up before his congregation and *muse*.   Meditation has its place, but should come before sermon-time.

Here is where the genius of the incarnation applies. For, if the minister were to consult himself alone, and his own preference, he would spin out his subjective speculations; he would be " disquisitious," to use a word found in no dictionary, but which ought to be in the preacher's, with a sign up like that for bicycle riders—" This hill is dangerous."   (I believe there is such a word as " disquisitorial " which might do for a brief, pat word of warning.)

On the contrary, we in this country are to preach to business men in business communities, men who come to church Sunday morning feeling still something of the terrific excitement and pressure of the week's industrial rivalries.   And the Spirit of the Incarnation will lead us to waive our tone of the doctrinaire, our abstractions and refinements of fancy, while retaining truth and refinement, and so pour the best of ourselves and of the truth of Christ into a certain form and manner derived from our industrial age, with that direct, concrete, business-like method of address which will bring the truth home to business men.

Now this means cost to the preacher ; but the cost means power, and power to save.

4th.   Thus, almost before he knows it, the preacher will find himself inhaling the stimulating air of what I have ventured to call the fourth great feature of the new age, viz. :—the New Philanthropy. And what again is this? It is, if I do not mistake, the scientific spirit, the social spirit and the industrial spirit, all blended together and touched, beyond their own knowledge, with the Spirit of Jesus, for the ministries of intelligent compassion and rescue. Here is the summit of our four-stepped modern terrace.

There is appearing among us a great and sane altruistic passion, the most wonderful thing in our age, which, steadily searching back of misery, seeks with science to find and with practical enterprise to heal the sources of it. To realize how this new and intellectual but Christian altruism is even now spreading in the world, is like finding a new bank of keys on an old, vast organ. A man who preaches in this spirit will not be "preaching to yesterday, or about yesterday," to quote Dr. Greer's apt phrase in his lectures on "The Preacher and his Place," but he will make yesterday and to-day and to-morrow as of one piece, one broad and living present. He will walk with his Christ between the church and the hospital. It is in this fresh union of Christ's altruism with modern intelligence, heat and light together, that we escape from the tyrannies of obsolete forms, reenter into the sense of Christ's own freedom and living power, and in our turn reach that in man which is perennial and immortal.

In each of these four inter-related and progressively ascending fields, then, that of scientific criticism, of social reconstruction, of industrial enterprise and of the new philanthropy, we discover that the chief elements in the life of the modern time are of God, are of Christ, and offer to the preacher the noblest material and method.   But let it be said with final emphasis that not until we combine these factors and regard them in their wonderful interaction and composite unity, do we find breaking upon us the full glory of the relation of this age to preaching, for we shall discover that this very interaction is most favorable to the union of true art and sacramental devotion in the pulpit.   Time does not permit the full elucidation of this subtle and superb fact.   But it is a fact beyond question.   "In hoc signo vinces."   For, on the artistic side, if I mistake not, art in this age, under the influence of these four tendencies of which we have spoken, is seeking, as never before, to be vital rather than merely formal.

Criticism is driving art back to reality, not indeed to the mere "fanciless fact," to use Browning's phrase, but to that large reality a part of which is the movement of the inner spirit.   And this is true all along the line of literary, as well as pictorial and plastic art.   The entire art spirit of the age is becoming inoculated with a certain noble, intense sense of the claim of life upon it.   A preacher now, therefore, as never before, can cultivate true art without losing hold on real life.

At the same time, on the other hand, and in the higher scale, this age, beyond any other age since the apostolic, is worthy to be called the age, the arena, the very "Cathedral" of the Incarnation, in this sense, that the minds of thinking men and of Christian men are more than ever turning towards this truth of the Incarnation as the solvent of problems, the master-note in philosophy and the key to Christian history and to Christian life—

> " Which shall to all our nights and days to come
> Give solely sovereign sway and masterdom." [1]

It comes to this, therefore, that from the union of these currents of modern feeling, an atmosphere is created in our age, which the true preacher finds exactly fitted to stimulate him to his best work, both in the artistic and the sacramental planes. He is not driven in upon a fraction of himself. His best power is drawn out in many directions. The same stroke which makes for his truest manhood makes for his finest ministry. When most in sympathy with the age, he is most stirred up to preach to it.

It is impossible to put this truth too strongly, although we do well to remember that wise line in the Proverbs—"He that hath knowledge spareth his words." But let me venture again to assert that the scientific, the social, the industrial, the humanitarian tendencies, interacting, create almost a new and splendid language, in which, with a nameless sense of exhilaration and free power, the preacher can sound and cry aloud the glory of the gospel truth. He discovers with a kind of amazement that when in the broadest way he can realize the genius of the time, he is in the best mood for preaching Christ to the time.

Why, gentlemen, the very latest science itself is approaching the reverential in its new temper towards the unrolling greatness of its vistas. The reverent silence of science in front of the newly apprehended

[1] " Macbeth."

vastness of its God, is by crude religionists mistaken for skepticism. Science investigating Nature must at last come up to Jesus, who stands at the summit of Nature, integral with it, yet "God manifest." Philanthropy studying humanity must also at last come up to Jesus as "the Christ"—the Saviour of men. The age is thus coming to our Christ and, carrying Christ in our heart, we, on our part, run forth to meet the age. How to find *in* the age—how to make *from* the age a new "body of Christ," becomes instantly our fascinating, absorbing errand.

The attempt to do this, to take what is most characteristic in modern life as a new and brilliant dialect in which to state once again *Christ* and Christ's changeless, ever-living truth—this attempt, carried steadily through the years, produces in the preacher a certain habitual glow, an alert mental attitude and action, in which free intellect blends with spiritual chivalry, and which is the finest possible mood for preaching itself.

Pardon a closing word to guard against misunderstanding. For any truth so fine as this is bound to have its counterfeits, and clever counterfeits, too. And so along our public ways and even our church aisles, perambulate the many *simulacra* of this great, simple thing we have been talking about. We behold the illuminati of every craze, the acolytes of esoteric cults, all of them using something of this very language concerning "reincarnation," some of them calling themselves "Christian," and some "scientific," while others try for a mixture of both, without much of either.

All these high-stepping people lack one thing and that is humor. They lack another thing and that is symmetry. They lack still a third thing most of all, and that is humility. They all say that they are "led by the Spirit." They all talk of a "Higher Life." Thus they steal the nomenclature of the true heavens, and some of them are really very noble in aim while mistaken in method. The vital fault with them all is that, without knowing it, they are putting *substitution* in place of genuine *incarnation*. On a higher and more truly Christian level something of the same error occasionally appears. Perhaps even certain of our honored brethren of the "Keswick" and "Northfield" schools of thought are not quite careful enough to guard this point. We need the Greek sense of open air perspective transferred to the spiritual life,— the Greek sense of health, fitness, harmonious proportion, realized in the moral and spiritual ideals. The higher life is the higher use of the lower life. The attempt to *substitute* the sacred for the secular is not so divine as the attempt to put the sacred *into* the secular. The genuine incarnation is *blood red* with human vitality. It turns not away from common, natural things and thoughts, but pours the Divine Spirit, without loss thereof, into common sense, into current life, into secular adaptations, into natural laws, into good humor, justice, candor, charity.

Apprehending these things, the true preacher is himself kept from such counterfeits as have been indicated. He is kept from pride and from a mawkish and stilted professionalism, as well as from that undue specialism which is the bane of the preacher. He is

kept large minded, sweet tempered, sane and practical. He neither emphasizes form above the spirit,
nor, on the other hand, emphasizes the spirit to the
neglect of the form, which of the two is the subtler
sin. Always it is the vital rather than the professional
which he seeks. He discovers that what the age is
hungering for and searching after is truth in forms of
justice and love in forms of beauty, and he knows that
in his Christ is this very union of divine " truth and
grace." That union he himself also strives to suggest
in at least some far-off hint thereof by his life and
preaching.

Does this ideal seem too difficult, too high for us,—
almost unattainable? I would avoid the impression
that an impossible ideal for the preacher is set up in
these simple addresses.

Let us be reverent and humble. Our Master ac-
complishes most of the "attaining" for us. "Not
that I have already obtained, or am already made perfect," cries the veteran Paul, "but I *press on.*"

Ah, great Apostle, thou dost lead a long procession
of us in that! We only "*press on*,"—archers only
(with the shot falling short) but archers *at* something divinely grand. Let us with really roused mind
do our full best; that is all. Leave the rest to the
unseen forces which are not only supplementing our
own, but are within our own, even as our Lord prom-
ised. Only if we do our best this week, let us next
week do still better. For even the great incarnation
of God in Christ Jesus was an incarnation into a
growth, in which babyhood precedes childhood and
the child the man.

LECTURE V

THE PREACHER OF TO-DAY PREPARING HIS SERMON

LECTURE V

THE PREACHER OF TO-DAY PREPARING HIS SERMON

It is not, as must be again emphasized, within the purpose of these addresses to repeat any portion of that elaborate code of professional rules concerning the preparation of sermons which you already have at hand in volumes upon this subject by the great masters of the art; and as to the preparation of *individual* sermons, the homiletic technique remains, even at the present moment, essentially the same as ever. In no profession, probably, has the distinctive note of technical preparation for special effort so little changed.

But when we apply our principles to the *general field* of sermon preparation, we become aware of certain new features of method especially suited to our own time. Two or three of these I will venture to suggest to-night.

And yet I have the deepening feeling that the best success in preaching is scarcely an affair of rules at all. Art in preaching is too vital to allow artifice. And when we go on from the idea of art to that conception of preaching which has been at the heart of these discussions, and regard it, in the soul of it, as a genuine incarnation, a reembodiment, under human limitations, but in timely forms, of the very Spirit and Message of the Master, then we perceive how the mere empirical rule must fail. Read such a book, for example, as the very interesting "Lectures on the History of Preaching," by Dr. Broadus,[1] and one is almost startled to learn how equal successes in this field have been associated with pulpit styles, denoting an almost infinite variety in manner of address. And there is good reason in this, for Nature's distinctive stamp on a man is most evident when that man is at his best, and in the pulpit a man must be at his best or fail. The truer the man, therefore, the more his style of preaching will be his own. The "Dii majorum gentium" of the pulpit are as unlike each other as are the books of the Bible, and yet as like. In no other field, accordingly, is the mere imitator so sure of ignominious failure as in preaching, and the pity of it is that even these failures do not seem to deter the fresh imitators.

What I shall say, therefore, must not be taken as insistence upon any rule, but as a hint towards certain features of method which our general argument emphasizes.

First. And first, may I say, *have several sermons in course of preparation at once.* For, according to our argument, the main thing in preparing the sermon is to prepare the preacher,—to make the preacher at the same time with making the sermon. The important result to be secured is not the production of a particular sermon, but is the production of a man

[1] Lectures on the "History of Preaching," by John A. Broadus, D. D., LL. D., Professor in the Southern Baptist Seminary, Louisville, Ky.—N. Y., Armstrong & Son, 1896.

who can preach. *He* is to be the sermon. And
the best preparation for his first five sermons is
that which continued for five years will make him the
best preacher. Not only is some particular tune to be
played, but the harp itself is to be strung and tuned
and set in the way of the winds of God. Now the
practice of having several sermons in hand at once is,
for many men certainly, the best way to realize this
large errand. One must not restrict one's self to the
comparatively petty object of preparing next Sunday's sermon during the week before. In the multi-
farious duties of the modern ministry, much time cannot be spent on every sermon. But the preacher
should always be spending much time on *some* sermon.

Let the modern sermon builder have the light dis-
patch boat and the ironclad battleship both building
at once. Let him select a great theme and put out
his utmost strength upon it for a month, two months,
subjecting that sermon to merciless reforging, trying
it by the three norms of style spoken of in our second
lecture, rewriting it half a dozen times. Let him cut
every bit of padding out of it, for one way to be at
least approximately interesting is to leave out what is
conspicuously dull, and if that process reduces us to
the mere text and "Amen," the frank statement of
that fact will certainly insure a large congregation the
next Sunday. But what with fresh ingathering and
then winnowing away, let the man make this particular
sermon the most athletic and finished thing he can
produce; while, at the same time, current sermons
are also prepared more briefly with a lighter hand, by
a simpler and swifter method.

You say this will result in inequality. Certainly. The most finely educative forces in our day do not result in mechanical equality. Emerson's famous quatrain applies not unaptly in this realm of the preacher :

> " There is no great and no small
> To the Soul that maketh all;
> And where it cometh all things are,
> And it cometh everywhere."

Sermons are not pieces of a long roll of bread,—exactly the same length of piece cut off every Sunday. The real sermon is the symphony of forty sermons. The particular inequality which, in the course of years, contributes to the noblest symmetry on the whole, is best both for the congregation and for the preacher. Your people will very soon find out what you are at, and will respect the resolute energy of your effort to make yourself the best preacher you can be.

But then, after your great sermon is finished, the Lord will probably humble you in your own eyes. You will very possibly experience a whimsical discomfiture, and find your magnificent effort outclassed in practical effect by what will come to you in the sudden inspiration of the moment. The point, however, is, and the law is, that such sudden flash from God is prepared for and made possible for you by just this patient, valiant hammering at the professional forge.

Second. In preparing these various sermons employ purposely *different styles of handling*. No man knows at first what his best style is. If he finds out in five years he will do well. St. Paul himself tried

experiments.   He said to the Corinthians that he became " all things to all men."   Only we must bear in
mind that the area of St. Paul's experimenting was
determined by the object he had in view.   This was
to save men.   "I am become all things to all men
that I may by all means save some."   The force of
the passage is in the *conjunction*, as also in the corre-
lated phrase in the context, "that I might gain "
(1 Cor. 9: 19–22).   The Apostle reiterates the phrase
like a blow.   Five separate times in this same connection
he repeats it, indicating how varied was his method,
and yet how the variety was dominated by the one
errand of gaining men.   So now, if a preacher excuses
himself for a kind of loose *ad captandum* variety in
method by saying he is making himself " all things to
all men " and stops there, his position is contemptible.
Our errand is not to amuse, but to save.   But it is to
amuse or anything else so far as it will save.

Now, in order to secure this flexibility of adaptation,
we must put ourselves under a training for various
styles, or rather for a method in style which admits at
once of outward variation with inner consistency.   So
only will the preacher fulfill that fine maxim of the
" Phaedrus "—(the latter half of which, by the way,
the preacher may as well read once a year) and "speak
or act about rhetoric in a manner which will be ac-
ceptable to God."   What the preacher is striving for
is to make himself, not all at once, but as soon as he
can, Christ's true artist in speech, Christ's own spokes-
man before the people, in their dialect of thought—a
master of expression in forms which will win and save.
Do not then crystallize, at least do not ossify too soon

into a given style, for such a style, caught up crudely at first, will be apt to become "cumbered with much serving," ponderously didactic, lacking lightness, as though one had *sat* on his loaf of bread.   Keep the intellectual fleet lightly moored—swinging a little at anchor.   Try half a dozen styles, only maintaining vital unity of purpose.   Temporary failure, here or there, matters little.   I remember a remark of Henry . Ward Beecher, "No man succeeds who doesn't dare to fail."   The man's finest and best style will at last be a certain spontaneous coincidence of a dozen partial approximations, each of which will have seemed to him half a failure.

Third.   Nevertheless, steadily, insistently, seek to secure, and as soon as possible, that style which is *best for you*, and best for the modern mind to which you speak.   We had best use our best as we go along.   As was argued in our second lecture, style—the form of a noble art for the preacher,—has its vital root in the philosophy of the Incarnation itself.   It is truth in forms of beauty, earnestness in forms of grace.   And we must not put off the endeavor to secure that one among these forms which for us is most natural and vital.

The books are full of delightfully contradictory instructions upon this matter of style, and no wonder, for I suppose that style is very much like a man's gait in walking, or the way he sits his horse in riding. How can a short man do it in a tall man's way? Then, too, style is a thing of paragraphs as much as of sentences.   It is the rhythm of mental march.   It resides not in a single quality, but in a synthesis of qualities.   One would say it is the product, first, of a man's general mental attitude, and, secondly, of his action from that attitude.   The mere stringing together of truths is not style and is not preaching.

Style for the preacher is, I repeat, a kind of chivalry.   It is soul.   It is the whole man's free force flung gallantly into genial expression.   One should write so that when not reading the phrase, but saying it as if extemporaneously, in the rush of swift speech, it will be his own most natural way of expressing himself.   And then, beyond that, we must dare still to believe that style relates to that which is of the living essence of the Beauty of God, a part of the order of Eternal Truth.

Style is nothing short of a divine thing, and when your impatient friend remarks that "you are too sedulous about the mere form of the thought," he is to be regarded with a gentle tolerance and a wonder how he can forget that the form of the thought is a part of the thought, and that a similar criticism could be directed against the very method of the Incarnation itself.

The philosophy of the Incarnation, and of the higher art as well, acknowledges the eternal worth of form in the sacred relation of form to beauty and of beauty to truth.

Fourth.   But not to stay too long upon these altitudes, let me say in more practical vein that all this involves the use of no rhetorical stilts.   The method of sermonizing must be simple.   Stilts are the worst sort of crutches.   It is much better to speak simply about something that is interesting than to speak tremendously about something that is not interesting.

You will remember Goethe's raillery in "Faust"—

> "And when you've something earnest to utter,
> Why hunt for words in such a flutter?
> Yes, your discourses, that are so refined,
> In which humanity's poor shreds you frizzle,
> Are unrefreshing as the mist and wind
> That through the withered leaves of autumn whistle." [1]

Let us enter the minister's study when a sermon is to be prepared. How shall he begin it? He must indeed be roused and alive; but he must begin simply. There is but one real rule as to beginning a sermon. *Begin where the people are.* The sermon should have saliency at the start, but saliency with naturalness.

Do not content yourself with what you write down easily enough in a lazy, "logy" hour ("Logy" is a "local United States word," according to the dictionary, but it means what I mean). Accept nothing as a constituent element of your real style which is not the product of roused energy in free action. The mood of the time is intense and practical. Nothing tame will match it. Get stirred all through by something fine. Then, having fired up the mental furnaces, pile in the crude ore, turn on the blast, cram down the gate, shut the blaze in, let the ore melt, so that the good metal may pour forth all at once,—glowing, liquid iron. In that mood, write rapidly; dash along. Never mind correctness. For the moment, forget rules. If my honored friend, Professor Merriam,[2] will pardon me, I would say, toss

[1] "Faust" Brook's translation.
[2] Professor of Practical Theology in Hartford Seminary.

even homiletics out of the window.   Pour everything
into expression, just as it naturally comes,—thought,
emotion, passion, the entire real manhood of you, all
quiveringly alive on the page.   Then, two days after,
beg Professor Merriam's pardon, summon him in,
take your scissors, and with his help correct the ex-
travagances of your work.   You will cut away a
third of it, half of it, only you will not cut the life of
it away, and it will be alive.

Successive approximations of this kind, pursued
with as definite and unrelaxing purpose as that with
which an oarsman trains himself to row, will, little by
little, reveal to a man his own best intellectual *gait*,
for the purpose of reaching the minds of men to-day.
He will learn that particular succession of intellectual
phases, his mind's *march* through which constitutes
his *style*.—Thenceforward, let him throw the accent
on this method which for him is best, but even then
not be tied to it.

We ministers, I suspect, are sometimes, without
knowing it, buried in our own seriousness, entombed
in mere dull didactics, of which people nowadays are
impatient, in which there is neither noble art nor any
true embodiment of the graceful and holy genius of
the Christian Incarnation.   We are literally *dead* in
earnest.   John the Baptist was serious and in earnest
but, speaking reverently, we may say that he had not
the divine *style* of the Nazarene.   This is not irrever-
ence.   It is putting style where it belongs in the rubric
of the preacher, viz., on the highest possible plane,
where is revealed that beauty of truth in the grace of
Christ, which we seek, as preachers, the re-rendition of

some little touch, if it may be, of the divine charm, wherein is the essence of the gospel.

I once called to see a minister. His wife said I could not see him, as he was "buried deep in his sermon." I happened to hear that sermon afterwards and I thought she told the truth. The man's mind had become so absorbed in its own gravity that it had unaware turned right round on itself and it was standing with the back of its head to the congregation when he preached.

Here, then, arises the question, which is the better, the written or the extemporaneous method for the preacher of to-day? I would venture to answer— both, each, all. The books give diverse answers. Shall we not rather say one method for one man, another for another. One for one period in a man's life, another for a later. One for one congregation, one occasion, another for another. A man should train himself in both methods. Lamp oil alone will not create the sermon. The question of paper or no paper has little to do with the vitality of preaching.

Some men read as though they spoke, and some men speak as though they read. Phillips Brooks, in some vital respects the noblest preacher of our generation in this land, read as though the paper were blazing in front of him. Conversely, any man, if really roused, can say on the spur of the moment what is better than the poorer half of what he will write.

The preacher ought to be ashamed to be a slave of any method. He is to make himself master of his art,—not at once, but after ten years, twenty years of steady, resolute, consecrated drill. At the end of that time, with paper or without, he ought to be ready and able to face any congregation, with much or little immediate preparation, in the name of his Master, with God's good news of spiritual rescue.

The best monograph on extemporaneous preaching is Dr. Storrs' now famous little book—"Preaching without Notes." But even that is not certain to make every man another Dr. Storrs. Dr. Storrs was the greatest pulpit orator of our epoch in this land,—the Cicero of Congregationalism. His mind was two minds in one. In one lobe it was facile and fluent as quicksilver, branching in every direction, and every fragment a perfect globule; while yet in the other lobe it was as insistent upon consecutive logical progress as is the shining sweep of a mighty river. But Dr. Storrs formed his extemporaneous style by a steady quarter century with the pen.

The late Dr. Shedd,[1] in his book upon "Homiletics," remarks very felicitously that the word "extemporaneous" should be construed, not from the "particular instant" but "from *all* the time, past as well as present." If the subject "possesses" a man, if he knows his theme, what he wants to say, and especially what he wants to do with and for his congregation, then the main conscious effort of the preacher will be to keep himself *en rapport* with those to whom he speaks, making them to think his thoughts, and to feel as he feels. Yet the young preacher will make a mistake, if instead of urging what is interesting and vital to himself, he utters

[1] Shedd's "Homiletics," p. 219.

merely what he may think ought to be interesting and vital to his people.

One secret, no doubt, of success in extempore address is to have absolutely in mind the practical end sought to be secured with the congregation. Avoid too many subdivisions. Let two-thirds of what you think you might say go unsaid. Then with a few main branchings or sub-topics of the theme also clearly in mind, let there be a swift rush of evident mental progress through those topics, in the spirit of the theme to the practical end. If ten minutes suffice for that, then let the preacher take his seat at the end of his ten minutes. He will not have exhausted the subject or the congregation either, but he will have made a good extempore sermon for the men of our time.

When a student, I once preached in a church in Connecticut. After I had finished, a deacon I knew —and nobody but a Connecticut deacon could have done it—said to me: " Well, brother, I think you have about exhausted the subject—as well as the congregation ! " I took the next train.

Do not, then, tell all you know or attempt to exhaust the field of theology in one sermon.

I believe the best general idea of manuscript help for most men in preaching to-day is that of the " brief," as the lawyers would say,—an outline, more or less complete, of what the man intends to deliver, with some parts perhaps written out in full, and with careful literary finish, and other parts just " blazed through," as the lumbermen say in going through a new piece of timber, so allowing the freest play to the inspiration of the moment when facing the audience. The people will very probably like the "blazed" parts best.

Pascal remarks in his brilliant little fragment on "The Art of Persuasion"—"The best books are those which those who read them believe they themselves could have written." So, we may almost say, the best sermons are those which those who hear them believe they themselves could have preached,—so essentially important is clearness and simplicity and a mutual good understanding between preacher and hearer. The manuscript, if it be much in evidence, is apt to obstruct this quick-current of mental fellowship.

On the whole, if I were to start in my profession over again, I should make most of my manuscripts "briefs" of sermons. One advantage is that if kept they do not take up so much room twenty years afterwards.[1]

Fifth. Confining our attention now to a given sermon, I would say, do not attempt to prepare more than one formal sermon a week, but prepare *yourself* to preach twice, if necessary, or even more. In other

---

[1] Just a hint here as to the use of manuscript in the pulpit. The best method I have ever discovered (and I *had* to discover it—necessity in that case was the mother of invention), is so variedly to distribute the crow tracks of one's writing on the page as that the *mere sight of the page*, or of *two or three largely written or underscored "catch words"* on it, will recall to one's memory the *entire page;* so that you can have your sermon entirely written out, and yet read it so that nobody will know that it is written.

words, always let sermon-making be the vital training of the power to preach, as well as the production of a particular discourse.

It is a good rule to begin the sermon very early in the week and make the entire week's work contribute to it, not necessarily in a formal, explicit way, but dynamically, if I may use the word. "A man may write at any time, if he will set himself doggedly to it," said old Sam Johnson. Our time is varied, tumultuous, insistent. We must grapple with it, we must match it. Therefore, let us make the entire current of every-day thought and life, newspapers, magazine literature, hard reading in the study, social visits, parish calls, prayers by the dying,—the entire orchestration of the week, glad and sad, to tell in the sermon, not merely in the way of furnishing for it material, but as imparting to it tone, cadence, vital response to the environment.

The preacher should and can and must thus live the homiletic life in the twentieth century. The total richness of the entire week should be put into that vivid thirty minutes in which on Sunday the personality of the preacher wrestles in God's name with the personalities in the congregation. Thus only can he reincarnate his ancient message in the dialect of the time.

If, therefore, the theme and main outline of the sermon can be secured as early as Tuesday night, or Wednesday noon, so much the better. The hardest part of any work is in rousing oneself to begin it. Let that initial scrimmage with the devil of laziness be over with, then, as early as possible. Allow no

Monday dawdling. Go fishing, if you want to be apostolic, but don't dawdle, even in fishing.

Monday morning is a good work time for many ministers. The stimulation of the day before keeps up in the brain. Beecher used to say that Monday was one of his best days. Tuesday was the " sag " day, the off day for him. Then, too, let the preacher not be afraid to bring his freshest professional reading during the week into his sermon, not formally, of course, in the way of scholastic or literary parade, but vitally. Command four hours every day for hard work in the study and put two of those upon the sermon or sermons. Bring into the sermon also the *pastoral* impressions of the week,—the fresh currents from the parish life. Gentlemen, never relinquish pastoral visitation. You will be tempted to do so, and you cannot do as much in this field as ministers could in former times, but, to a real extent you can and should maintain the practice. You must care for others all your life, and care to care. Pastoral visitation keeps the minister human ; it puts a certain humanly sympathetic quality into his preaching which is indispensable. Only conduct such visitation not carelessly, but nobly, tactfully, homiletically, so to speak, and make it tell, not in the way of crude and bald allusions, but by imparting subtle, delicate fragrances and cadences to the sermon.

The deep reason for all this, according to the principles we have urged, is that the sermon is simply the culmination of the preacher's entire ministry. It is the pastorate vocalized. It is the week-day manhood set to Sunday utterance.

We must keep ourselves human, and all the more human because we are ministers. You remember what was said of Phillips Brooks, that " he was a saint, but was so human that one didn't mind it." Laugh with your people and weep with them and be so much of a man and friend that both laughter and weeping shall be real. God loves laughter if it be the laughter of love. There is a fine and genial humor which even in the pulpit has its place. There is a gaiety which is born of the Resurrection. Know your people's homes and speak to those homes on Sunday. If some fond mother asks you to come in and see her baby and you think you have no time for parish babies in the twentieth century, remember Jesus among the little ones and go. And then put, not the incident surely, but some gentle, pure touch, caught from motherhood and from yonder Judean uplands, into your sermon.

Sixth. Yet, notwithstanding these injunctions as to bringing everything into the sermon, I urge in the next place, that we cultivate most diligently the *art of rejection,* which lies at the bottom of the art of perspective in sermon writing, in our day especially. We cannot incarnate our message for the men of our time in any other way. Never an age so impatient of superfluous luggage as ours. All noble art, indeed, begins with rejection. Cut away all the marble which is not statue.

> " The more the marble wastes
> The more the statue grows,"

said Michael Angelo. Retain in the sermon only

what "*has to be*" there,—to employ our rifle shot idiom. Above all, do not *dally* with rhetorical conceits. Strike once, and get on. Do not hammer the head off the nail. "Continued eloquence wearies," said Pascal,—a maxim which you eloquent young men would do well to remember.

Says Southey—"If you would be pungent, be brief." (A maxim the present lecturer has evidently forgotten.) "It is with words as with sunbeams," he continues, "the more they are condensed the deeper they burn." And that modern master of style, Robert Louis Stevenson, remarks :—"To add irrelevant matter is not to lengthen but to *bury*." We write and speak under fire. Let us get out of ourselves and back of ourselves and realize beforehand the standpoint of the hearer. Always ask yourself the question which lies back of the one you are asking the people,—the question which the people will probably be asking themselves, as to what you are saying. Remember the point that commands the point you are looking at. Don't go on too long in any particular strain without taking yourself to task. Side with the supposable critic against yourself. To quote our Emerson again—"Ride on the horse that is chasing you."

All this will be found to involve that subtle and profound yet masterful spirit of intellectual self-denial which, as we have seen, lies so near the heart of preaching, both as an art and an incarnation. Brethren, the cold truth is that in our sermon writing we put in too much that we might leave out. Thus we lose both push and perspective. We bear on too

hard all the time, and thus lose the sense of real urgency altogether.   You remember the French *mot*—
"You can do anything with a bayonet except *sit* on
it."   When we think we have made a point we sit
down on it.   We camp there.   In this continuous
emphasis we lose emphasis.   We lose style.   We lose
art.   But we lose something deeper, namely, the tone
of the spiritual beauty of Christ's Truth.

Let us emulate the light, sure touch of the Master.
We content ourselves with what is even for us the
second rate in our preaching, without asking whether
the sermon and the people also cannot get on just as
well without it.   Write nothing except what you cannot help writing.   Ten minutes' fine work is better
alone than with another ten minutes' poor work tacked
on.   Lumber is not life.   We should leave in the sermon nothing but what is alive, and alive as Christ
would have it alive.   People nowadays want your
best, then done with it.   Retain only what is freshest,
and truest to yourself, in your sermon, and you will be
fresh and true to your people, and it is a great com-
fort to remember that the congregation does not know
what we *leave out*.

Therefore, comrades, let us not reiterate over much.
We shall not avoid platitude, but let us, by the grace
of Heaven, avoid vociferation in platitude, and especially avoid vociferating the same platitude twice in
the same sermon.   God save us from oracular intensity
in commonplaces !

And when we are through let us stop.   Modern
people prefer that even Hamlet's soliloquy should not
"go on forever."   I knew a minister, of whom it

was said that he lacked only one thing, and that was "terminal facilities!"

Here is where we secretly must needs "cut off the right hand" in making sermons. We have to deny ourselves in order to reembody the *grace* of the Lord. Have we ever reflected how much it may have cost Jesus even to speak in His simple, homely way, and in no other? Something that we have written may seem to us "fine," but we know it is out of proportion and out of place. Well, then, leave it out—let it go. That sheet will light the kitchen fire, but it is not the best agent for representing the sane symmetry, the natural grace of our holy Message. If a man finally saves for his sermon one-half of what he writes for it, he will do well. I speak now of the earlier years in which he is drilling and fitting himself as a preacher.

Shall one then polish for the sake of polishing? God forbid. Many sermons have to be snap-shots,—done quickly, with a free hand. The preacher toils over style with motive similar to that with which the telescope-maker toils days and days to impart those last, little, delicate touches to the great glass. Why? To make the glass smooth and pretty? How childish! It is to perfect the "figure" of the lens, so that the lens, itself unseen, shall accurately and with perfect achromatism reveal the infinite and immortal splendors in yonder distant skies.

Seventh.—May I venture then, in the simplest possible closing word, to suggest six qualities as specially apposite to the modern sermon? For whatever other qualities may be present, these six are insisted on by the modern mind and need.

Three of these are intellectual qualities. One is *clearness*. (If we talk about that point we shall make it less clear.) I may say, however, that as the practice of our journals illustrates, the clearness of main paragraph divisions suits the modern habit of mind. Distinct title, the pith of the thing in a head-line, separate paragraphs, with not so many subdivisions as in this lecture,—this, together with logical connection, straight and plain, and swift movement right on, is what the modern mind asks for.

The second intellectual quality now called for is *interestingness*, to hazard a word employed by Herbert Spencer. That is, we must, on the way up to our ultimate end, speak of something interesting to people, else we cannot hold them. We must speak of what people are interested in, in order to interest them in what they ought to be interested in. This indeed was the method of Jesus Himself in His parables, and beneath it beats the deep genius of the Incarnation.

The third intellectual quality is what we may call *progressiveness*. That is to say, the modern sermon must "get on," to use our quick vernacular. It must have a target and reach it. Modern men are brought up on newspapers, and to this extent we may utilize the habit of mind which a journalistic age produces. We are then to incorporate in our work these three intellectual values,—clarity, interest and progress.

Then, above these are two moral qualities which are indispensable. They are sincerity and sympathy. The impression of these is to be made at the start of the sermon and continued till the closing syllable.

Treat the congregation as a company of friends, and so disarm it of any latent critical antagonism.

Then, still above these qualities even, is the one supreme and spiritual quality wherein is revealed, as we have been saying, my fellow-workers, over and over again, the holy shrine of our calling. I refer to the indescribable, vital impression of the presence of the Living God in our preaching, so that the people, though addressed in their own dialect and through our human personality, shall see and feel not us, but Him.

It is in this spirit that we reach the sermon's close. "That is not first which is spiritual," says St. Paul, "but that which is natural; then that which is spiritual." It is into the *closing third* of the sermon that the complete spiritual impression of the entire sermon must be concentrated. Here art is at its height, and yet is most forgotten. The preacher himself is most forgotten. He incarnates his message.

Not that this closing third need be continuously exalted in diction. It may be very varied in manner, now vehement, now clothed with an exceeding great gentleness, or again falling into quick, little, homely turns, or even be humorous, here and there. All that depends upon the man and the occasion and is as God wills. But whatever the mental modulation may be, this closing strain must glow throughout with a living and constant fire. A living fellowship pulsates through the preacher, between Him whom he speaks *for* and them whom he speaks *to*. Christ and the people are brought face to face.

As you are aware, in many conventional text-books this particular mood and strain of speech are supposed not to be secured until the moment of final utterance in the pulpit, as if hardly possible to be realized until called forth by the excitement of the public occasion.

My most earnest word to you to-day is that this mood of feeling and address should not be reserved, and need not be reserved for the public hour. It may be realized in the preacher's soul beforehand, in the privacy of his study, before God.

Is not this the mystery and this the blessedness of our Lord's living presence with us? I see the preacher turning even when alone into that sacred final strain. In preparing the sermon up to this point, he has endeavored to hew to the line. He has opened the Word of God. He has filled clear paragraphs with his own freshest thought. Following a plain track, he has pushed right on, not dallying upon side issues, but crowding forward swiftly with an orderly symmetry of plan. He has sought truth and grace. And thus, even beforehand, he comes to behold in his mind's eye the people massed before him. Then it is that the greatness of the coming moment humbles him. There sweeps into his view, like some great, gleaming orb, the higher sense of his calling,— the beauty of the soul, the Vision of the Lord, and he calls to himself, as if saying,—"Have I been preaching? Nay, I have been but standing on the threshold and in the vestibule of my privilege. Now I will *preach*, ere these my people go." Learning lays aside its air of superiority, and logic puts on the robe of manly entreaty. Everything in the preacher's

mind becomes alive and crowds up towards the production of one final impression.   Then ensues, by the
grace of God, even in the quietness of solitary preparation, that wonderful synthesis between message,
speaker and hearer, each at its best, which is the
unique glory of our calling.   A new spirit sweeps
over the man, not only as he preaches, but also as he
prepares himself to preach.   He becomes simpler, his
words are straighter.   He feels himself as in the presence of the King, and his brethren, the King's sons,
who may not know their birthright, are also before
him.   He must tell them of their heritage; he must,
if he may, embody something of the nobleness of that
heritage.   So he writes; not in monotone, even of intensity, but with homely, living phrase perhaps, or
with burst of metaphor, touch of pathos, flash of
passion, or with illumined spiritual intuition, or in a
clear calmness of the rational soul.   With any or all
of these modulations of the mind, as God has endowed
him, and with the wonderful chivalry of Christ's fellowship suffusing all, unifying all, so he will prepare
to speak, as well as speak.   So he will stand, when
the moment comes, a man among his fellows, yet
with the entire manhood of him made vocal and set
to the keynote of the Cross,—the living incarnation
of Christ's gospel in the form best suited to the time.

What is it like?   It is like a man's talk with his
friend concerning their Best Friend.   What is it like?
It is not altogether unlike Christ's Calvary and Resurrection.

Blessed be God, it is preaching to *save*, preaching
that will save, by Christ's Power and in Christ's Name.

THE PREACHER OF TO-DAY BEFORE HIS
CONGREGATION

LECTURE VI

THE PREACHER OF TO-DAY BEFORE HIS CONGREGATION

I wish, by God's grace, to strike no other note in this closing address of our course than that which was struck at the beginning.

Setting aside all attempt at academic formality, avoiding trespass upon the field of homiletics proper, as taught in the seminary curriculum, our aim was simply to present the subject of preaching as it appears from the standpoint of the theological student himself to-day. And our first assumption, therefore, was that most welcome one of faith in the student mind, and especially in its undertone, not only as the select product of these Christian generations, but also because those who are now students in our seminaries are the very men who are already set apart and called of God to the leadership of our churches in the land in the coming generation.

The student himself, therefore, we summoned to be the real lecturer. His impression of the New Testament ideal of preaching we accepted as truly interpretative, and we listened to him, as in the cogent language of his two-score interrogatories he disclosed what he felt preaching should be,—an art which led up into an incarnation, and which in turn, addressing itself to the present age, singled out its finest factors, in which also the life of Christ is moving, such as the spirit of critical investigation, the spirit of social fellowship, the spirit of industrial enterprise, the spirit of intelligent philanthropy,—and by combining such selected features of the time, found in them a new dialect, a new form of expression, in which he, as Christ's minister, might again reproduce, without loss, the Gospel Message.

In the previous lecture, in the attempt to apply these principles upon the direct field of sermon preparation, the discussion fell away a little, I thought, from the high level of attention to the principles themselves. Possibly this was unavoidable in an address devoted solely to practical suggestions; but to-night, let us renew and urge our loftiest conception of the holy calling. And this the more distinctly because we now draw together all our threads of reflection around the consideration of that final moment, so brief yet so noble, when, after due preparation, the preacher stands at last face to face with his congregation.

First. In a simple and swift order of thought, let us ask, in the first place, what *is* the modern church audience, the modern congregation?

It is a formidable creature, yet fascinating. We should not be afraid of it, but understand it and respect it. Familiarity with this spectacle recurring every Sunday has dulled our minds to the sense of its unique greatness, for here really is the supreme arena where the modern spirit, child of the modern age, is confronted by the Eternal, as disclosed from ancient days in the Gospel of Jesus Christ.

This is surely not an over-strained fancy. The

dramatic grandeur of the scene we easily miss, no doubt, but the preacher should feel it, and continue to feel it. Nothing else in the modern world exhibits the same grandeur. At no other point of modern life does the spirit of the past at its best so accurately meet, so vitally wrestle with the spirit of the present. It was a famous saying of Tholuck, which Dr. Stalker reproduces in his lectures, that "a sermon ought to have heaven for its father and the earth for its mother."

Even the surface aspect of the typical modern church congregation is remarkable, although any description of it seems a platitude. It is an eager, hurried, critical, sensitive mass of humanity, all in its best clothes indeed, and presumably in its best spiritual form also, and yet appealing very deeply to sympathy,—a thousand souls of every class, occupation, mental aptitude,—a throng heterogeneous enough, yet strangely unified in the rushing torrent of our modern life, as trees, dissimilar, bend evenly, like brothers, in a gale.

Naturally you will reply that the Sunday audience does not fairly represent the age, but is a slice cut horizontally rather than vertically from it, and undoubtedly certain isolated phenomena of our time are not disclosed within church doors. In the church is probably the larger proportion of what is worthiest and best in the community, while, on the other hand, the dregs of society, the riff-raff, the outlaws, are not seen in the churches; nor are certain of the hyper-cultivated and agnostic classes seen there; nor is the man-about-town seen there.

But when one remembers the rapid rush of waters in our human tides to-day, how the bottom of society is in two generations or at most three, thrown to the top, and how large a proportion of every community at some period of life drifts within the sanctuary, one must conclude that, in a large way of putting it, the church assembly is a very fair microcosm of the modern world. Here are business men, professional men; here are families; the rich and the poor; capital and labor meet. Take it all in all, what we face in the modern congregation is the age itself, both devout and defiant, both believing and sceptical, volcanic in energy, perturbed even in repose, seeking any amusement as a relief from strain, volatile in sensations, lashed by ambitions, more conscious of the present than thoughtful for the future, passionately alive, though now hushed because it is Sunday, driven by forces novel and splendid, through efforts it cannot stop to measure, toward ends it will not lift itself to see.

Not that the congregation itself is conscious of all this, or feels the electric coil which it is wearing. On the contrary, the average worshipper, as he enters the church on Sunday morning, is perhaps rather apathetic. The week's storm and stress is succeeded by the Sunday calm. He is disposed to observation and criticism, rather than to effort or devotion.

Yet the whole constitutes a strangely pathetic spectacle when one looks at it narrowly. Here are people trying to forget. Here are comedies without merriment, and tragedies without dignity. Here is humanity careless of its glory and callous as to its shame. Here are grand men and grander women, beaten down by the flail of misfortune. The people are decorous. They bow; they stand; they sing,— some of them, if the choir will give them a chance; they are outwardly attentive. The real mental mood is somewhat quiescent, possibly even somnolent. It is a day of coolness after the hot week. Here and there are a few really roused, religious minds, but the average tone is conventional, united with a vague seriousness. It is the vast, roaring, week-day world, arresting itself for the moment, and trying, rather dimly, to remember that it ought to remember eternity.

Now, gentlemen, I repeat, all this is of course platitude. These features lie plainly on the surface and are seen easily. I refer to these patent aspects of the modern congregation, only for the sake of saying that, important as they are, they constitute by far the *lesser half* of that picture of the real congregation which the preacher must have vividly before his mind.

The preacher, it is true, must mark these superficial aspects, and understand them accurately, else he cannot deal with them; but he must, with far more commanding intensity, realize before his mind's eye an invisible audience which lies within and beneath the audience visible.

For a church audience is two audiences. One is this self-conscious, modern, visible congregation. But beneath this is another, unconscious of itself, or only semi-conscious. You have, of course, perceived the thought before I have expressed it. This invisible hearer within the visible one is the continuing humanity in every man, the true product of the past.

There is an immortal voyager whom somehow we find already in our little boats when we take them. It is the undertone in every man in which is the residuum of the ancestral generations, the rich sub-soil of Christian civilization.

Herein is the deep mystery of the human soul, which is " from of old." Within yonder church-goer who seems so superficial, so careless, is a man of latent sensibilities, impulses, yes, and faiths, too, which however dull or critical the man is at the moment, perpetuate in him the essence of ancient creed and choral, the fragrance of ancient sacraments, the reverberation of old heroisms—the valor and patience of Christian centuries. There is a unique and solemn splendor in the fact that each individual is a kind of flask or crucible into which all the generations have poured something of their best.

This is not a fancy, though I am putting it rather fancifully. It is scientific truth, certainly. " Even these highest of our mental faculties," remarks Haekel, "are just as much subject to the laws of heredity as are their respective organs."[1] Social science recognizes a solidarity of the generations. A thousand noble choices, brave conflicts, nameless endurances, beat on in this modern blood and brain. And there is a further truth also, which science hesitates to state. This invisible audience within the visible is the humanity which Christ Himself has touched and is still touching in subtlest, holiest ways. So we as Christians must believe. This is not "idealizing" the

---

[1] " Riddles of the Universe," Ernst Haekel.

congregation. It is discerning the real, full truth respecting it.

Now, the commanding fact for the preacher to realize is this invisible and spiritual element in his audience. He must remember that behind what his eye sees is that which his mind may see, wherein resides a sure responsiveness to God's truth. To count upon that latent responsiveness is the way to freedom and to fearlessness, to roused sympathy, to vital mastery in addressing the congregation visible. For with this invisible man Christ Himself also is evermore pleading. The Kingdom of Christ is already begun in him. The Lord's Prayer, the Triune Benediction, the deep, old creed phrases, "I believe in God, the Father Almighty, and in Jesus Christ, his only Son, our Lord," the "Gloria," the "Te Deum," the "holy invocations" at the Christening, the Holy Communion, the bridal, the burial,—these have recorded themselves in the very substructure of the mind of the modern hearer, in the most intimate and instinctive turns of cerebral process and spiritual aspiration. They can be counted on; they can be appealed to; and in the midst of them, as upon congenial soil, we can again set up the Cross of the Incarnation.

Now, all this apprehension concerning what the congregation really is and stands for, must be entertained by the preacher, not as a pleasing fancy, an amiable dream, but it must be realized with a distinct, athletic grasp, so that his whole mind and manner shall be flooded with it.

Here again opens before us the unmatched distinction of our great vocation, that at its summit of professional duty it involves this large sense of humanity, this grasp upon the whole of the living, human creature, in which is an emancipation from the fetters of fear, a vision of the battalions behind the battalions, a vital affiliation with the deeper and more controlling forces of the soul.

Second. What then, in the second place, is the effect upon the preacher of so realizing humanity in the congregation? The answer has already been intimated. The effect is indescribably inspiring. It is, if I understand aright, such as to justify, to call out and to maintain that precise mood in the man, that all-round, roused energy, sympathetic with the environment, yet independent of it, and charged with a divine message to it, which we have endeavored to describe as the true and effective mood for the preacher. Here the light flashes back upon all the path of thought we have travelled through these lectures. The moment of final utterance corresponds with the path that leads up to it.

The congregation realized in its dual unity inspires the preacher to fulfill at once that double function of noble artist and true prophet, which beforehand he had set before himself as the loftiest ideal of preaching. Art is requisite in order to deal with the audience visible. No art is too accomplished to be brought to this task; while at the same time the noble, sweet, chivalrous manhood, in which Christ Himself can be in some sense reincarnate, appeals to and reaches the audience invisible.

Thus you discover that the *whole* man in the pew matches your own finest thought of speech to him. Herein is joy and power. The preacher is made independent, and yet full of that genial grace which is often the blossom of the most rational and devout earnestness. If I know that a stranger is really my brother, though he himself is unaware of the fact, what a peculiar, unfearing courtesy flows into my manner towards him! If in a foreign land I meet a man whom I happen to know was cradled under the stars and stripes, though he is ignorant of it, what a proud, glad comradeship on my part pervades our interview, though he perhaps persists in opposing me or criticising me! I am saying to myself all the time— 'O my dear fellow, how differently you will feel when I can get you to know that the same gun and flag boomed and waved over our babyhood, and that even on a foreign shore we are kindred still.' Such a sentiment completely emancipates the preacher from that terror of the critical spirit in a congregation, which to all of us is apt to be so paralyzing.

It seems to me that something like this must have been in the *tone* of Jesus speaking to men, and we want to reproduce that same attitude and tone, so far as in our poor way we can.

The most remarkable pulpit genius of our time once said to me—"Lyman, do you know what my deepest feeling is when I face my great audience?" "No," I said, "may I ask what it is?" Said he, "Compassion. Ah," he continued, "we must be endlessly, incredibly compassionate!" He was looking at the invisible congregation as well as the visible.

Now, this roused mood from which the preacher thus launches his sermon, tells not only upon the power of the sermon, but upon the constant power of the minister in all his work. What people desire in their minister is not a Sunday performer, but a *man whom they can trust* seven days in the week,—trust in living and trust in dying—a man whom they can "tie up to," as the phrase goes,—a man who incarnates his gospel, who is, in his way, the thing he asks them to be in their way.

People want reality, but not only that. They want a reality in the preacher which shall elicit the nobler reality in themselves. And this large way of realizing what I have called rather fantastically both the visible and the invisible congregation, passes over into that very character in the preacher, out of the pulpit as well as in it, which the people *can* "tie up to" and trust.

I cannot, gentlemen, by any words at my command, adequately indicate my sense of the indispensable and noble value of this generic mood of mind in our vocation. There is in it a certain excellent charm and power, an indefinable reproduction of what everybody at the bottom of his soul believes in,—the beautiful truth of Christ. It is a mood of faith and of joy, at once athletic and winsome, alive with practical sympathy and efficiency, and yet in its depths glowing with the chivalry, almost unworldly, of a man who speaks for the Man who spoke for God.

Third. As to utterance itself:—May I venture upon two or three practical hints? See, for example, that the right physical conditions exist. Go to bed early Saturday night. No late dinners out, no fascinating and enchanting social calls Saturday night, young

gentlemen!—no exhausting professional duty, either.
Let us take lessons from the oarsman. Come up to
Sunday morning rested and fresh. Then, a cool bath,
a light breakfast, a brisk, short walk, or ten minutes
with the dumbbells and clubs, and you are "in con-
dition." Do not "fuss" about the sermon. Glance
at the notes, perhaps; do not "work" over them.
You will have help. Christ cares more than you do
that you should preach well. One thing I might suggest: go alone for a half hour before preaching and
devote that half hour to *naming over* your people, in
a keen, kind way, one by one. That, and a gentle
uplook at the Christ for whom and with whom you
are to speak—and you are ready. For a man may,
with a certain serenity and almost gaiety of trust, approach even the supreme effort of his life, for the psychology which underlies this is the law of God in the
soul, the truth of the indwelling Spirit, the relation of
conscious human power to the inspirations from on
high.

Then go into the pulpit strung, but simple, realizing
the congregation you see and also the congregation
you see that Christ sees, determined to do your best
as a soul-wrestler, a life-saver, and ready also to sacrifice in a second your finest page, if it gets in the way
of the on-going march of your people's responsiveness.

Then, as you begin in the sermon, do not start too
far above the ground. Even on the ladder that
reaches to heaven it is not well to stand half-way up
the ladder above your people's heads. In any case,
start with them. Look at them. Make them feel
that you care for them, and for what you are doing.

As to gesture, manner, and all that, God forbid that one should lay down rules. Art is present, the finest. But the time to think about art is not when you are preaching. I know only one real rule for that moment;—get fully roused and into sympathy with the congregation and then forget yourself and be natural. It is a mistake to be natural when you are dull, because the result of that will be simply a most incredible prosiness. The idea of Demosthenes' famous definition of oratory is fully roused manhood in the free play of natural action. Let the eloquent world speak through you. Let the flash of passion come like the lightning, when it will. Let us pray against monotony. If people get sleepy, tell them something interesting that they did not know. Do not be afraid of humor. Anything in heaven's name, so that it really be in heaven's name, is better than listlessness.

Then, too, the entire sermon from beginning to end must glow with the impression of fellowship with the people,—not a mawkish sentimentalism, but a genuine and manly fellowship. Nothing else is Christian. I do not mean that invective, or satire, what Wendell Phillips used to call "the rich vocabulary of Saxon scorn," has no place in the pulpit. Indignation, if noble, is a part of legitimate pulpit fire, but it must be reserved for rare occasions and for that which is clearly deserving of it, so that you may carry your congregation with you, even when you denounce its sins or satirize its follies.

In this kindled mood, at once humble and uplifted, which may outwardly be very quiet, there is a kind of wireless telegraphy, almost telepathy, between your congregation and yourself, so that as you sweep on and up and become subjectively intense and a little in danger of losing your audience, you are called back to them,—you introduce little turns and changes, put in grappling irons, allusions, illustrations, almost colloquialisms, perhaps, not at all premeditated or written down. Then, as the sermon goes forward toward its close, it becomes simpler, swifter, straighter. The supreme tones may come in, tenderness, pathos, spiritual exaltation. But you will remember that the genius of the incarnation is not to stay up on Mount Pisgah, but to carry the spirit of Mount Pisgah down to the Plains of Jericho, and the banks of the Jordan.

If the sermon is extemporaneous, do not try to say what is not in your mind, but say what is in your mind. Extemporaneous preaching is not trying to summon something that you have not been thinking of, but it is trying to tell something that you have been thinking of. Everything should be pervaded by the air of natural appropriateness.

Fourth. From the summit thus attained, let us look back once again upon that living group of your forty-four questions which have followed us through all our discussion, like a band of marching men. In a formal way we shall, perhaps, no more articulate these questions to each other; for I should have to say to-night of these lectures what my Spanish guide at Burgos said to me when I lost the train—" When is the next one?" I asked. "Signor," he replied, "there is no next one!" Our paths diverge to-night, and you, with your fresher morning strength will crowd on ahead of us with whom it is noontide or afternoon.

And yet we shall none of us quite bid good-bye to these questions. They sprang from the hearts of true men and they will follow us through the years.

Have these interrogatories been answered? In a literal way, no. In a mechanical, technical way, no. In that way they cannot be answered. An alleged answer of that sort would fail under practical test. In a more vital fashion some attempt has been made by way of answer. More than half of the questions have been directly brought up and quoted as we have gone forward in our discussion; and the entire discussion from beginning to end has been shaped with reference to them, and has sought to honor the spirit which pervades them. But because the questions themselves sprang from life, they can be answered only through life. If Christ's minister can attain— and by Christ's grace he can attain—unto a certain *spirit*, a certain habitual attitude and action of mind, such as we have endeavored to describe, then I must believe the questions will very largely answer themselves.

But you will observe that even then the details of the answers will vary for different men.

Question number 4, for example—"How much 'apologetics' is needed in the present pulpit?" None, or very little, in a technical sense. The line of debate has shifted. Let professors, critical experts fight the needed battles of apologetics. Do you proclaim the gospel in such winsome, manly fashion as shall make it seem to need no defense.

Or take question number 23—"What should be the relation of the preacher to social problems and political issues?" One would answer that question very differently for different men. Yet the underlying principle is plain for all, and the same for all. Our relation to these "burning questions," as they are called, should be intelligent, fearless, practical; and we should speak of them sometimes, but not as experts. We may and should apply to them or to certain phases of them the principles concerning which we ought to be experts—the living and eternal principles of Christian ethics. But, brethren, we ministers do not know as much about these matters of current economics as we think we do, or as many other people do. Let us not expose our sermons to criticism similar to that of Macaulay upon Atterbury's defense of the alleged "Letters of Phalaris," that it "was the best book ever written upon the wrong side of a subject, of both sides of which the author was profoundly ignorant."

I turn again to your questions as I close, with continued wonder at their practical insight and vital power.

Question 11—"How can one preach a system of doctrine?" By preaching *Christ* all up and down the scale of life, from God to little children. A Living Christology is the final result of a Biblical theology, and is the best form for the popular statement of that theology. Shall the minister then have no dogmatics in his sermon, no effort at theological instruction? I do not say that. To say it would be disrespect to the educational challenge of this age; but I say, present your theology in living rather than in merely speculative forms.

Question 13—" How can the effect of sermons be made cumulative ? "   By being a growing man yourself.

Question 14—" Does modern preaching emphasize the human side of Christ too much ? "   No ; but it does not emphasize the "Immanuel" in Christ enough.

Question 15—" What has become in modern preaching of the personal appeal to the unconverted ? "   It is shifted back to where Jesus put it in His attitude towards parental influence and little children.

Question 19—" What will rally to the church a larger percentage of men ? "   A finer manhood in the pulpit.

Question 25—" How shall one get personal experience into sermonic form ? "   First, have the experience, and then if it be real you cannot help putting it into your sermon, but it will be done easily, naturally and without parade.   Anything that is *hard* to do in that line is not worth doing.

Question 26—" How can a man find the common ground between himself and the congregation ? "   By finding the common ground between his Master and the congregation.

Question 43—" Can a man definitely count upon receiving special aid from on high in addition to the natural powers of his own mind ? "   Yes, but only in connection with his own best use of those natural powers.

And then those two great questions which run through half a dozen special interrogatories in the series, to which allusion has already been made —

"What truths are most effective in preaching?" We have answered before, and I would answer again, —those in stating which the best synthesis is possible between Christ, yourself, and your hearer. And, "What resources and powers in the mind are worth the most in preaching?" I would answer, those which are the best agents for producing and realizing this synthesis.

And now, gentlemen, my simple but to me delightful task is done. I must not sin against my own canons of utterance and dally at the close, nor pile up words as though some ambitious finale could make good the defects in what has been said. I have to thank you for your courtesy, as I also thank you more than you can know for providing for me the basis upon which these addresses stand.

I have sought nothing save the most direct address I could command to the members of these classes. I have not turned apologist, nor have I turned critic. Nor have I sought to pass judgment upon living men or current methods. I have assumed, as such lectures in this place must assume, faith in the New Testament and in its master—truth,—the truth of "Christ crucified," but risen and alive and actually in the world and with His people.

From the standpoint of the mere rationalist, the thought that pervades these lectures, that preaching is an art which finally forgets itself as it leads up to a true reincarnation of the Gospel Message in the Power of a Living Christ, is, of course, a devotee's dream. But I am addressing not rationalists, but Christian students, and as such you "believe and are persuaded " that the doctrine of " Christ with us," is not a dream.

At the same time we have tried to breathe the true air of the modern time itself, its thought, its purpose, its free and splendid life. For, if I do not mistake, we have not had in mind a mystical, esoteric conception of our vocation, but one sane and Scriptural. Nor is it one which works toward conceit and spiritual pride. I commend to you a view of our calling which invokes that large and symmetrical culture found in the incessant mental interplay between the rational, practical, modern spirit, and the loftier intuitions which perpetuate the faith of the Christian ages. I congratulate you upon a calling in which the impulse of a noble art, seeking to express truth in forms of beauty, is led thereby to the moral beauty of Jesus Christ Himself, and becomes a passion to reproduce that beauty, to reincarnate it in forms suited to the time,—forms which may win and save. And thus, whether the older conceptions of Christianity, those represented by the irenic orthodox consensus, contain the truer view of it, or whether the more modernly humanitarian conceptions of Chrisianity be the truer, in either case, as I conceive it, the essential argument of these lectures stands.

And for you, if you will pardon a personal word as I leave you, it is with a kind of fraternal solicitude which I cannot dwell upon without seeming weakness, that I look along the vista of the years and see your efforts, your disappointments perhaps, but also your sure triumphs. Sometimes we fail. More and more perhaps we shall think we fail. But occasional failure to a true man is worth almost more than success, because it teaches him more. We must learn to fling up our burden and let it rest as on a shelf in the Crag of God.

God with you, comrades. God give you steadiness and swiftness. Do not set too much store by any man's ideas, *even your own*. These simple talks of mine, for example ; fling them aside if they do not match with what for you is truest. We all have our personal equation, and a sum in substraction is necessary before we accept any man's ideas. Yet trust your deeper self. Dare to fling yourself out upon that which seems to you surely true. This was the way of our Master, and He will not condemn even His mistaken child, who tries in sincerity and humility to follow His method.

Be genial toward books, toward thoughts, toward men. But go up for your *orders* only to Christ and to the higher terraces of your own spirit. Let us be alive and stay so. "Who grasps the moment as it flies," you remember Goethe's line—" he is the real man." Keep up the splendid jet of roused and ready power in nerve and blood and brain, only mingle with it the holy sacrifice of prayer, and so be God's man, Christ's man in the midst of the vast and tossing time. The true preacher is, in all his life, and in every day of it and detail of it, dominated by this one passion, namely to *be* the kind of man he asks others to be,—to incarnate his message.

We are on the verge of yet more signal exhibitions of the divine power. The twentieth century is to be, I believe, even more evidently than the nineteenth, Christ's century. The critical era is to be succeeded by the constructive. The sectarian is to give way before the fraternal. *Christian federation* is to be the great note of the coming decades, whose advancing bugles we hear through the defiles of the mountains. What a glorious reveille will be summoning you, young men, when others will be answering the evening roll call!

A profound change is coming over the face of the waters. One meets it among the ablest and most earnest younger scholars and Christian workers everywhere. Its note is, in a word—*Realize Christ and get together in Him.* The new spirit is a faith that works by love and purifies the heart. The agony of the long fight against unbelief is lessening before the profoundly rising tide of faith in the reality of Immanuel and His Kingdom. I hold to this nobler reading of the closing movement of the old century. The genius of the Incarnation includes not only the Cross but the Resurrection.

Let us not fear to be conservative in the sense of conserving that which the ages have found best worth preserving. *Construction*, in Christ's name, is the true note. And in the practical field this reverently constructive temper is to be matched by a new sense of human fellowship in the same Supreme Name. Divisions will remain, but they will be divisions in the same marching army. The army is the thing. Sectarianism will be forgotten folly. Live men are to work for live men in God's strength, in Christ's truth, and hand in hand.

So, brothers, fare you well. Preach in love. Preach to save. Make the most of yourselves, for

God will do His part towards making the most of you. The thing to maintain is *spiritual chivalry.* No theory of the Bible or of doctrine or of church which fails to secure this will stand. Christ is the Master-Truth, the Master-Power. In Him, fare you well.

We will stand for the irenic and for the fraternal. We will refuse to be side-tracked, either on the " Old School " or the " New School " rails. God grant His blessing upon any institution which endeavors to be in the best sense both conservative and liberal, which, having guarded the precious chalice of the ancient faith even to the sunset of the old century, yet lifts that very chalice into the dawn of a new morning. The old and the new together ! The old in the forms of the new ! For that let us stand.

And the " evening and the morning " shall be " one day," and in that day shall be builded on the earth the true City of God, " coming down from God out of heaven,"—a city of just thoughts and kind deeds, of allied communions and saved men, wherein shall appear in ever brightening glory the tender and majestic Presence of " Him that was slain,"—our Brother, walking with us still, as in the old Syrian time, yet our Master, our Redeemer, " on whose Head are many crowns," " Whose Kingdom shall have no end."

The Fact of Christ

By
P. Carnegie Simpson, M.A.

12mo, Cloth, $1.25

"SOMETIMES it is so impressive that it seems as if the risen Lord must be present with the reader."—*N. Y. Observer.*

" It lifts the reader high above the tenuous mists of drifting doubts."—*Interior.*

" Packed with helpful and practical thought, wonderfully well suited to the religious needs of our times. It is a message which reaches the very core of vital Christianity and is admirably adapted to confirm faith. The author admirably meets the agnostic and skeptical tendency of our day."—*The Advance.*

"To read Mr. P. Carnegie Simpson's finely developed argument is a rare and enjoyable treat. The crispness and raciness of the style are the fit accompaniments and expression of clean, logical processes and thoroughly digested thought . . . The bare statement of this, of course, conveys no idea of the wealth of the book, sparkling as it is with brilliant sayings, and yielding at every point suggestive hints or fresh solution of the perennial problems. The book as a whole makes it apparent that we have among us a a strong and independent thinker, who sees deeply and clearly."—*Dr. Marcus Dods.*

"Distinguished both for intellectual clearness and keenness and for moral courage."—*The Outlook.*

" He writes with a force and keenness of expression which at times rise to the epigrammatic."—*Sunday School Times.*

" It is a new and forceful statement of the fact and claim of Christianity. To me it is one of the finest statements of the Atonement principle that I have ever read."—*G. Campbell Morgan.*

" By a strong and independent thinker who sees deeply and clearly"